Java Question Bank For Beginners: MCQs, Short Answer, Practical & Long Answer Questions

Anshuman Mishra

Published by Anshuman Mishra, 2025.

BOOK TITLE:

"JAVA QUESTION BANK FOR BEGINNERS: MCQS, SHORT ANSWER, PRACTICAL & LONG ANSWER QUESTIONS"

ABOUT THIS BOOK:

"JAVA QUESTION BANK FOR BEGINNERS" IS A COMPREHENSIVE QUESTION BANK SPECIFICALLY DESIGNED TO HELP NEW LEARNERS OF JAVA MASTER THE FOUNDATIONAL CONCEPTS OF JAVA PROGRAMMING THROUGH PRACTICE. UNLIKE TRADITIONAL TEXTBOOKS THAT FOCUS ON LENGTHY THEORY EXPLANATIONS, THIS BOOK IS ORGANIZED IN A QUESTION-ANSWER FORMAT THAT FOCUSES SOLELY ON HELPING BEGINNERS LEARN THROUGH PRACTICE.

THE BOOK IS DIVIDED INTO CHAPTERS BASED ON KEY JAVA CONCEPTS, INCLUDING BASIC SYNTAX, CONTROL FLOW, OBJECT-ORIENTED PROGRAMMING (OOP), ARRAYS, STRINGS, EXCEPTION HANDLING, JAVA COLLECTIONS, FILE HANDLING, AND MORE. EACH CHAPTER IS STRUCTURED WITH FOUR DISTINCT TYPES OF QUESTIONS:

- **MULTIPLE CHOICE QUESTIONS (MCQS):** THESE QUESTIONS HELP TEST YOUR KNOWLEDGE OF JAVA SYNTAX, CONCEPTS, AND BEST PRACTICES IN A QUICK AND EFFECTIVE WAY.
- **SHORT ANSWER QUESTIONS:** THESE QUESTIONS ENCOURAGE YOU TO SUMMARIZE KEY CONCEPTS IN JAVA. ANSWERING THESE QUESTIONS WILL HELP YOU UNDERSTAND AND REMEMBER THE MATERIAL.
- **PRACTICAL QUESTIONS:** THESE HANDS-ON CODING QUESTIONS ALLOW YOU TO PRACTICE WRITING JAVA CODE. WORKING ON PRACTICAL PROBLEMS IS ESSENTIAL FOR UNDERSTANDING HOW TO IMPLEMENT THE CONCEPTS YOU HAVE LEARNED.
- **LONG ANSWER QUESTIONS:** THESE COMPREHENSIVE QUESTIONS PROVIDE YOU WITH THE OPPORTUNITY TO EXPLAIN JAVA CONCEPTS IN DETAIL, HELPING SOLIDIFY YOUR UNDERSTANDING OF CORE TOPICS AND ALLOWING YOU TO DEMONSTRATE YOUR LEARNING IN-DEPTH.

THIS BOOK IS SUITABLE FOR BEGINNERS WHO WANT TO BUILD A SOLID FOUNDATION IN JAVA PROGRAMMING. WHETHER YOU ARE PREPARING FOR EXAMS, INTERVIEWS, OR SIMPLY LEARNING FOR PERSONAL GROWTH, THIS QUESTION BANK SERVES AS AN IDEAL COMPANION TO ENHANCE YOUR LEARNING EXPERIENCE.

WHAT YOU WILL GAIN AFTER READING THIS BOOK:

1. **THOROUGH UNDERSTANDING OF JAVA BASICS**: BY ANSWERING MCQS AND SHORT ANSWER QUESTIONS, YOU WILL GAIN A STRONG UNDERSTANDING OF JAVA'S BASIC CONCEPTS, INCLUDING SYNTAX, VARIABLES, OPERATORS, AND CONTROL STRUCTURES.

2. **PRACTICAL CODING SKILLS**: THE PRACTICAL CODING QUESTIONS WILL ENABLE YOU TO DEVELOP HANDS-ON CODING SKILLS, WHICH ARE ESSENTIAL FOR BECOMING PROFICIENT IN JAVA. YOU WILL LEARN TO SOLVE REAL-WORLD PROGRAMMING PROBLEMS, PREPARING YOU FOR TASKS YOU MAY ENCOUNTER IN PROGRAMMING JOBS.

3. **IMPROVED PROBLEM-SOLVING ABILITIES**: THIS BOOK WILL HELP SHARPEN YOUR PROBLEM-SOLVING SKILLS BY GUIDING YOU THROUGH A WIDE VARIETY OF QUESTIONS, FROM SIMPLE TO COMPLEX. YOU WILL LEARN HOW TO BREAK DOWN PROBLEMS AND COME UP WITH EFFECTIVE SOLUTIONS USING JAVA.

4. **DEEP UNDERSTANDING OF CORE JAVA CONCEPTS**: THE LONG ANSWER QUESTIONS WILL ENCOURAGE YOU TO EXPLAIN JAVA CONCEPTS THOROUGHLY. THIS DEEPENS YOUR UNDERSTANDING AND ENSURES THAT YOU NOT ONLY KNOW THE SYNTAX BUT ALSO UNDERSTAND HOW AND WHY THINGS WORK THE WAY THEY DO IN JAVA.

5. **CONFIDENCE FOR EXAMS AND INTERVIEWS**: THE DIVERSE RANGE OF QUESTIONS (MCQS, SHORT ANSWERS, PRACTICALS, AND LONG ANSWERS) WILL PREPARE YOU FOR ACADEMIC EXAMS, CODING TESTS, OR JAVA-RELATED INTERVIEWS. PRACTICING WITH THIS BOOK WILL BUILD YOUR CONFIDENCE WHEN TACKLING REAL-WORLD JAVA PROGRAMMING CHALLENGES.

6. **CLEAR GRASP OF OBJECT-ORIENTED PROGRAMMING (OOP)**: OOP IS A CORE CONCEPT IN JAVA. THROUGH THIS BOOK, YOU WILL GAIN A SOLID GRASP OF OBJECT-ORIENTED PRINCIPLES SUCH AS CLASSES, OBJECTS, INHERITANCE, POLYMORPHISM, ENCAPSULATION, AND ABSTRACTION, ALL OF WHICH ARE VITAL FOR WRITING EFFICIENT JAVA CODE.

7. **FAMILIARITY WITH JAVA'S ADVANCED FEATURES**: AS YOU PROGRESS THROUGH THE CHAPTERS, YOU WILL ALSO GAIN INSIGHTS INTO JAVA'S ADVANCED FEATURES SUCH AS EXCEPTION HANDLING, COLLECTIONS, AND FILE HANDLING, WHICH ARE ESSENTIAL FOR WRITING ROBUST AND SCALABLE APPLICATIONS.

8. **STRONG FOUNDATION FOR FURTHER LEARNING**: BY MASTERING THE CONCEPTS IN THIS BOOK, YOU WILL ESTABLISH A STRONG FOUNDATION IN JAVA, ENABLING YOU TO EXPLORE MORE ADVANCED TOPICS IN JAVA DEVELOPMENT, SUCH AS GUI PROGRAMMING, NETWORKING, DATABASES, AND MORE.

HOW TO STUDY THIS BOOK:

1. **FOLLOW THE CHAPTERS SEQUENTIALLY**: IT IS RECOMMENDED TO STUDY THIS BOOK CHAPTER BY CHAPTER, AS THE CONCEPTS ARE BUILT PROGRESSIVELY. STARTING FROM THE BASICS AND ADVANCING THROUGH EACH TOPIC WILL ENSURE THAT YOU LEARN JAVA IN A LOGICAL AND STRUCTURED MANNER.

2. **SOLVE THE MCQS FIRST**: BEGIN EACH CHAPTER BY ANSWERING THE MCQS. THIS WILL HELP YOU TEST YOUR INITIAL KNOWLEDGE OF THE TOPIC AND HIGHLIGHT AREAS YOU NEED TO FOCUS ON. MCQS ALSO HELP WITH QUICK REVISIONS AND REINFORCE WHAT YOU'VE LEARNED.

3. **ANSWER THE SHORT ANSWER QUESTIONS**: AFTER COMPLETING THE MCQS, ATTEMPT THE SHORT ANSWER QUESTIONS. THESE ARE DESIGNED TO ENCOURAGE YOU TO WRITE CONCISE EXPLANATIONS AND SUMMARIZE IMPORTANT CONCEPTS.

4. **PRACTICE THE PRACTICAL QUESTIONS**: ONCE YOU'RE COMFORTABLE WITH THE THEORY, MOVE ON TO THE PRACTICAL QUESTIONS. THESE QUESTIONS WILL HELP YOU IMPROVE YOUR CODING SKILLS AND GET HANDS-ON EXPERIENCE WITH JAVA SYNTAX AND PROBLEM-SOLVING.

5. **WORK ON LONG ANSWER QUESTIONS**: LONG ANSWER QUESTIONS ALLOW YOU TO ELABORATE ON THE CONCEPTS YOU HAVE LEARNED AND HELP YOU UNDERSTAND JAVA AT A DEEPER LEVEL. THESE WILL BE PARTICULARLY HELPFUL WHEN PREPARING FOR EXAMS OR INTERVIEWS THAT REQUIRE DETAILED EXPLANATIONS.

6. **REVIEW YOUR ANSWERS**: AFTER ATTEMPTING THE QUESTIONS, REVIEW YOUR ANSWERS AND SOLUTIONS TO IDENTIFY ANY AREAS WHERE YOU MAY NEED IMPROVEMENT. THIS WILL HELP REINFORCE THE MATERIAL AND GUIDE YOUR CONTINUED LEARNING.

7. **PRACTICE REGULARLY**: JAVA IS A SKILL THAT IMPROVES WITH CONSISTENT PRACTICE. SET ASIDE REGULAR TIME TO GO OVER THE QUESTIONS AND WRITE CODE. THE MORE YOU PRACTICE, THE MORE COMFORTABLE AND PROFICIENT YOU WILL BECOME.

8. **TEST YOURSELF**: PERIODICALLY, CHALLENGE YOURSELF BY SOLVING QUESTIONS FROM PREVIOUS CHAPTERS TO SEE HOW MUCH YOU'VE RETAINED AND HOW WELL YOU CAN APPLY THE CONCEPTS IN NEW SITUATIONS.

BOOK TITLE:

"JAVA QUESTION BANK FOR BEGINNERS: MCQS, SHORT ANSWER, PRACTICAL & LONG ANSWER QUESTIONS"

TABLE OF CONTENTS

ABOUT THE AUTHOR:

ANSHUMAN KUMAR MISHRA IS A SEASONED EDUCATOR AND PROLIFIC AUTHOR WITH OVER 20 YEARS OF EXPERIENCE IN THE TEACHING FIELD. HE HAS A DEEP PASSION FOR TECHNOLOGY AND A STRONG COMMITMENT TO MAKING COMPLEX CONCEPTS ACCESSIBLE TO STUDENTS AT ALL LEVELS. WITH AN M.TECH IN COMPUTER SCIENCE FROM BIT MESRA, HE BRINGS BOTH ACADEMIC EXPERTISE AND PRACTICAL EXPERIENCE TO HIS WORK.

CURRENTLY SERVING AS AN ASSISTANT PROFESSOR AT DORANDA COLLEGE, ANSHUMAN HAS BEEN A GUIDING FORCE FOR MANY ASPIRING COMPUTER SCIENTISTS AND ENGINEERS, NURTURING THEIR SKILLS IN VARIOUS PROGRAMMING LANGUAGES AND TECHNOLOGIES. HIS TEACHING STYLE IS FOCUSED ON CLARITY, HANDS-ON LEARNING, AND MAKING STUDENTS COMFORTABLE WITH BOTH THEORETICAL AND PRACTICAL ASPECTS OF COMPUTER SCIENCE.

THROUGHOUT HIS CAREER, ANSHUMAN KUMAR MISHRA HAS AUTHORED OVER 25 BOOKS ON A WIDE RANGE OF TOPICS INCLUDING PYTHON, JAVA, C, C++, DATA SCIENCE, ARTIFICIAL INTELLIGENCE, SQL, .NET, WEB PROGRAMMING, DATA STRUCTURES, AND MORE. HIS BOOKS HAVE BEEN WELL-RECEIVED BY STUDENTS, PROFESSIONALS, AND INSTITUTIONS ALIKE FOR THEIR STRAIGHTFORWARD EXPLANATIONS, PRACTICAL EXERCISES, AND DEEP INSIGHTS INTO THE SUBJECTS.

ANSHUMAN'S APPROACH TO TEACHING AND WRITING IS ROOTED IN HIS BELIEF THAT LEARNING SHOULD BE ENGAGING, INTUITIVE, AND HIGHLY APPLICABLE TO REAL-WORLD SCENARIOS. HIS EXPERIENCE IN BOTH ACADEMIA AND INDUSTRY HAS GIVEN HIM A UNIQUE PERSPECTIVE ON HOW TO BEST PREPARE STUDENTS FOR THE EVOLVING WORLD OF TECHNOLOGY.

IN HIS BOOKS, ANSHUMAN AIMS NOT ONLY TO IMPART KNOWLEDGE BUT ALSO TO INSPIRE A LIFELONG LOVE FOR LEARNING AND EXPLORATION IN THE WORLD OF COMPUTER SCIENCE AND PROGRAMMING.

"JAVA Programming code should be written for developers to comprehend, and only incidentally for the compiler to execute."

— Anshuman Mishra

Copyright Page

Title: JAVA QUESTION BANK FOR BEGINNERS: MCQS, SHORT ANSWER, PRACTICAL & LONG ANSWER QUESTIONS

CHAPTER 1: BASIC CONCEPTS OF JAVA

30 MCQs:

---

1. Which of the following is the correct syntax to declare a variable in Java?

a) `int 1x;`
b) `int x;`
c) `x int;`
d) `int x = 10;`

Answer: b) `int x;`

---

2. What is the default value of an integer variable in Java?

a) 0
b) null
c) undefined
d) NaN

Answer: a) 0

---

3. Which of the following is the correct keyword to define a constant in Java?

a) `constant`
b) `final`
c) `static`
d) `immutable`

Answer: b) `final`

---

4. Which of the following is a primitive data type in Java?

a) String
b) Array
c) int
d) Object

Answer: c) int

---

5. What is the size of an `int` in Java?

a) 8 bits
b) 16 bits
c) 32 bits
d) 64 bits

Answer: c) 32 bits

---

6. What is the value of the expression `5 + 3 * 2` in Java?

a) 16
b) 11
c) 13
d) 15

Answer: b) 11

---

7. Which method is used to start the execution of a Java program?

a) `start()`
b) `begin()`
c) `main()`
d) `execute()`

Answer: c) main()

---

8. Which of the following statements is true about Java?

a) Java is a low-level programming language.
b) Java is an interpreted language.
c) Java is a platform-independent language.
d) Java requires hardware-specific code to run.

Answer: c) Java is a platform-independent language.

9. In Java, which keyword is used to create a class?

a) `object`
b) `class`
c) `new`
d) `instance`

Answer: b) class

10. Which of the following is not a valid identifier in Java?

a) `myVariable`
b) `my_var`
c) `2ndValue`
d) `_value`

Answer: c) 2ndValue

11. Which of the following is used to terminate a loop in Java?

a) `break`
b) `exit`
c) `stop`
d) `halt`

Answer: a) break

12. Which operator is used to compare two values in Java?

a) `=`
b) `==`
c) `===`
d) `!=`

Answer: b) ==

13. What is the range of values for a `byte` data type in Java?

a) -128 to 127
b) 0 to 255
c) -32768 to 32767
d) -2147483648 to 2147483647

Answer: a) -128 to 127

---

14. Which of the following is the correct way to declare a constant variable in Java?

a) `int x = 5;`
b) `final int x = 5;`
c) `static int x = 5;`
d) `constant int x = 5;`

Answer: b) final int x = 5;

---

15. Which of the following is the correct syntax for a single-line comment in Java?

a) `<!-- This is a comment -->`
b) `/* This is a comment */`
c) `// This is a comment`
d) `# This is a comment`

Answer: c) // This is a comment

**16. What will be the output of the following Java code?

```
System.out.println(10 / 3);**
```

a) 3
b) 3.0
c) 3.33
d) Error

Answer: a) 3

17. Which of the following keywords is used to create an object in Java?

a) `create`
b) `new`
c) `instance`
d) `object`

Answer: b) new

18. What is the result of the expression `true && false` in Java?

a) true
b) false
c) 1
d) 0

Answer: b) false

19. Which of the following statements is used to skip the current iteration of a loop in Java?

a) `skip`
b) `continue`
c) `pass`
d) `halt`

Answer: b) continue

20. Which class in Java is used to read user input from the console?

a) `Scanner`
b) `InputStreamReader`
c) `System`
d) `Reader`

Answer: a) Scanner

---

21. In Java, which of the following is the correct way to declare a string?

a) `char str = "Hello";`
b) `String str = "Hello";`
c) `string str = 'Hello';`
d) `string str = "Hello";`

Answer: b) String str = "Hello";

---

22. Which of the following Java data types can store a decimal value?

a) `int`
b) `double`
c) `char`
d) `boolean`

Answer: b) double

---

23. What is the default value of a `boolean` variable in Java?

a) 0
b) `null`
c) `false`
d) `true`

Answer: c) false

---

24. What is the size of a `double` data type in Java?

a) 32 bits
b) 64 bits
c) 16 bits
d) 128 bits

Answer: b) 64 bits

---

25. Which of the following is used to create a new instance of a class in Java?

a) `new ClassName();`
b) `ClassName newObject = new();`
c) `new = ClassName();`
d) `object ClassName = new();`

Answer: a) new ClassName();

---

26. What is the purpose of the `System.exit(0)` command in Java?

a) To stop the program
b) To exit the current loop
c) To terminate the current method
d) To stop the JVM

Answer: a) To stop the program

---

27. Which of the following statements is used to declare a method in Java?

a) `method int add() {}`
b) `public int add() {}`
c) `def int add() {}`
d) `function int add() {}`

Answer: b) public int add() {}

---

28. Which of the following is the default value for a reference variable in Java?

a) `null`
b) `0`
c) `false`
d) `undefined`

Answer: a) null

29. Which of the following statements is true about Java?

a) Java supports multiple inheritance directly.
b) Java is not case-sensitive.
c) Java is a platform-independent language.
d) Java can only be used for web applications.

Answer: c) Java is a platform-independent language.

30. Which of the following methods is used to compare two strings in Java?

a) `equals()`
b) `compare()`
c) `equalsIgnoreCase()`
d) Both a) and c)

Answer: d) Both a) and c)

30 short-length questions with answers based:

1. What is Java?

Answer: Java is a high-level, object-oriented programming language that is platform-independent and used for building a wide range of applications.

2. What are the features of Java?

Answer: Some key features of Java include platform independence, object-oriented programming, automatic garbage collection, security, and multi-threading.

3. What is the purpose of the `main()` method in Java?

Answer: The `main()` method is the entry point of any Java application. It is the first method that the Java Virtual Machine (JVM) calls to start the execution of a program.

4. What is the default value of an `int` variable in Java?

Answer: The default value of an `int` variable is `0`.

5. What is the difference between `int` and `Integer` in Java?

Answer: `int` is a primitive data type, while `Integer` is a wrapper class for the `int` type, allowing it to be used as an object.

6. What does the keyword `final` do in Java?

Answer: The `final` keyword is used to define constants, prevent method overriding, and prevent inheritance of classes.

7. What is a variable in Java?

Answer: A variable in Java is a container for storing data values. It has a data type and a name that identifies it.

8. What is the difference between == and = in Java?

Answer: == is a comparison operator used to compare values, while = is the assignment operator used to assign a value to a variable.

9. What is a constant in Java?

Answer: A constant in Java is a variable whose value cannot be changed after initialization. It is defined using the `final` keyword.

10. What is the size of a `long` data type in Java?

Answer: The size of a `long` data type is 64 bits.

---

11. What is an array in Java?

Answer: An array is a data structure that stores multiple values of the same type in a single variable.

---

12. What is the use of the `this` keyword in Java?

Answer: The `this` keyword refers to the current instance of the class. It is often used to distinguish instance variables from local variables.

---

13. What is an object in Java?

Answer: An object in Java is an instance of a class. It contains data and methods that define its behavior.

---

14. What is a class in Java?

Answer: A class in Java is a blueprint or template from which objects are created. It defines properties and behaviors (methods) for the objects.

---

15. How do you create an object in Java?

Answer: An object is created using the `new` keyword followed by the class constructor, e.g.,
```
ClassName objectName = new ClassName();
```

16. What is inheritance in Java?

Answer: Inheritance is an object-oriented concept where a class can inherit properties and methods from another class. The class that inherits is called a subclass, and the class it inherits from is the superclass.

17. What is encapsulation in Java?

Answer: Encapsulation is the concept of bundling data (variables) and methods that operate on the data into a single unit, typically a class. It also involves restricting access to some of the object's components using access modifiers.

18. What is polymorphism in Java?

Answer: Polymorphism allows objects of different classes to be treated as objects of a common superclass. It can be achieved through method overloading and method overriding.

19. What is method overloading in Java?

Answer: Method overloading occurs when multiple methods have the same name but different parameters (either in number, type, or both) within the same class.

20. What is method overriding in Java?

Answer: Method overriding occurs when a subclass provides its own implementation of a method that is already defined in its superclass.

21. What is the purpose of the `break` statement in Java?

Answer: The `break` statement is used to exit from a loop or switch statement prematurely.

22. What is the purpose of the `continue` statement in Java?

Answer: The `continue` statement is used to skip the current iteration of a loop and continue with the next iteration.

23. What is the difference between `ArrayList` and `LinkedList` in Java?

Answer: `ArrayList` is based on a dynamic array, while `LinkedList` is based on a doubly linked list. `ArrayList` offers faster random access, while `LinkedList` provides better performance when inserting/removing elements from the middle.

24. What is the `null` keyword in Java?

Answer: The `null` keyword represents the absence of a value or an object reference. It can be assigned to any object reference type.

25. What is a constructor in Java?

Answer: A constructor is a special method in Java used to initialize objects. It has the same name as the class and does not return any value.

26. What is a `static` keyword in Java?

Answer: The `static` keyword is used to define class-level variables or methods that can be accessed without creating an instance of the class.

27. What is the difference between `String` and `StringBuilder` in Java?

Answer: `String` is immutable, meaning its value cannot be changed, while `StringBuilder` is mutable, meaning its value can be modified without creating new objects.

28. What does the `public` access modifier mean in Java?

Answer: The `public` access modifier allows the variable, method, or class to be accessed from anywhere in the program.

29. What is an interface in Java?

Answer: An interface in Java is a reference type that contains abstract methods. A class that implements an interface must provide implementations for all of its methods.

30. What is the purpose of the `super` keyword in Java?

Answer: The `super` keyword is used to refer to the immediate superclass of the current object. It is commonly used to call superclass methods or constructors.

10 practical questions with their solutions:

---

1. Write a Java program to print "Hello, World!" on the screen.

Solution:

```
public class HelloWorld {
    public static void main(String[] args) {
        System.out.println("Hello, World!");
    }
}
```

Explanation: This program uses the `System.out.println()` method to print "Hello, World!" to the console.

---

2. Write a Java program to find the sum of two numbers entered by the user.

Solution:

```
import java.util.Scanner;

public class SumOfNumbers {
    public static void main(String[] args) {
        Scanner scanner = new Scanner(System.in);

        System.out.print("Enter the first number: ");
        int num1 = scanner.nextInt();

        System.out.print("Enter the second number: ");
        int num2 = scanner.nextInt();

        int sum = num1 + num2;
        System.out.println("The sum is: " + sum);

        scanner.close();
    }}
```

Explanation: This program uses the `Scanner` class to take user input for two numbers, then calculates and prints their sum.

3. Write a Java program to calculate the area of a rectangle.

Solution:

```java
import java.util.Scanner;

public class RectangleArea {
    public static void main(String[] args) {
        Scanner scanner = new Scanner(System.in);

        System.out.print("Enter the length of the rectangle: ");
        double length = scanner.nextDouble();

        System.out.print("Enter the width of the rectangle: ");
        double width = scanner.nextDouble();

        double area = length * width;
        System.out.println("The area of the rectangle is: " + area);

        scanner.close();
    }
}
```

Explanation: This program calculates the area of a rectangle by multiplying the length and width provided by the user.

---

4. Write a Java program to check if a number is even or odd.

Solution:

```java
import java.util.Scanner;

public class EvenOdd {
    public static void main(String[] args) {
        Scanner scanner = new Scanner(System.in);

        System.out.print("Enter a number: ");
        int number = scanner.nextInt();

        if (number % 2 == 0) {
            System.out.println(number + " is even.");
        } else {
            System.out.println(number + " is odd.");
        }

        scanner.close();
    }
}
```

Explanation: The program checks if a number is divisible by 2 using the modulus operator (%). If the remainder is 0, the number is even; otherwise, it is odd.

---

5. Write a Java program to find the largest of three numbers.

Solution:

```java
import java.util.Scanner;

public class LargestOfThree {
    public static void main(String[] args) {
        Scanner scanner = new Scanner(System.in);

        System.out.print("Enter the first number: ");
        int num1 = scanner.nextInt();

        System.out.print("Enter the second number: ");
        int num2 = scanner.nextInt();

        System.out.print("Enter the third number: ");
        int num3 = scanner.nextInt();

        int largest = (num1 > num2) ? (num1 > num3 ? num1 : num3) : (num2 > num3 ? num2 : num3);

        System.out.println("The largest number is: " + largest);

        scanner.close();
    }
}
```

Explanation: The program uses the ternary operator (? :) to find the largest of the three numbers.

---

6. Write a Java program to display the multiplication table of a given number.

Solution:

```java
import java.util.Scanner;

public class MultiplicationTable {
    public static void main(String[] args) {
        Scanner scanner = new Scanner(System.in);

        System.out.print("Enter a number: ");
        int number = scanner.nextInt();

        System.out.println("Multiplication Table of " + number + ":");
        for (int i = 1; i <= 10; i++) {
            System.out.println(number + " x " + i + " = " + (number * i));
        }

        scanner.close();
    }
```

```
}
```

Explanation: The program uses a `for` loop to generate the multiplication table from 1 to 10 for the given number.

---

7. Write a Java program to reverse a number entered by the user.

Solution:

```java
import java.util.Scanner;

public class ReverseNumber {
    public static void main(String[] args) {
        Scanner scanner = new Scanner(System.in);

        System.out.print("Enter a number: ");
        int number = scanner.nextInt();

        int reversed = 0;
        while (number != 0) {
            int digit = number % 10;
            reversed = reversed * 10 + digit;
            number /= 10;
        }

        System.out.println("Reversed number is: " + reversed);

        scanner.close();
    }
}
```

Explanation: This program uses a `while` loop to reverse the digits of the number. It repeatedly extracts the last digit and appends it to the reversed number.

---

8. Write a Java program to find the factorial of a number.

Solution:

```java
import java.util.Scanner;

public class Factorial {
    public static void main(String[] args) {
        Scanner scanner = new Scanner(System.in);

        System.out.print("Enter a number: ");
        int number = scanner.nextInt();

        int factorial = 1;
```

```
        for (int i = 1; i <= number; i++) {
            factorial *= i;
        }

        System.out.println("The factorial of " + number + " is: " +
factorial);

        scanner.close();
    }
}
```

Explanation: This program uses a `for` loop to multiply the integers from 1 to the given number to calculate the factorial.

---

9. Write a Java program to check if a number is a prime number.

Solution:

```java
import java.util.Scanner;

public class PrimeNumber {
    public static void main(String[] args) {
        Scanner scanner = new Scanner(System.in);

        System.out.print("Enter a number: ");
        int number = scanner.nextInt();

        boolean isPrime = true;

        if (number <= 1) {
            isPrime = false;
        } else {
            for (int i = 2; i <= number / 2; i++) {
                if (number % i == 0) {
                    isPrime = false;
                    break;
                }
            }
        }

        if (isPrime) {
            System.out.println(number + " is a prime number.");
        } else {
            System.out.println(number + " is not a prime number.");
        }

        scanner.close();
    }
}
```

Explanation: This program checks if a number is divisible by any number other than 1 and itself to determine if it's prime.

10. Write a Java program to count the number of vowels in a string.

Solution:

```java
import java.util.Scanner;

public class VowelCount {
    public static void main(String[] args) {
        Scanner scanner = new Scanner(System.in);

        System.out.print("Enter a string: ");
        String input = scanner.nextLine();

        int count = 0;

        for (int i = 0; i < input.length(); i++) {
            char ch = input.charAt(i);
            if (ch == 'a' || ch == 'e' || ch == 'i' || ch == 'o' || ch == 'u' ||
                ch == 'A' || ch == 'E' || ch == 'I' || ch == 'O' || ch ==
'U') {
                count++;
            }
        }

        System.out.println("Number of vowels in the string: " + count);

        scanner.close();
    }
}
```

Explanation: This program iterates through each character in the string and checks if it is a vowel (both lowercase and uppercase), then counts the total number of vowels.

10 long-length questions with answers:

1. What are the key features of Java and how do they contribute to its popularity?

Answer:
Java is a high-level, object-oriented, and platform-independent programming language that offers several features making it widely popular:

1. **Platform Independence (Write Once, Run Anywhere)**: Java programs are compiled into bytecode, which is executed on any machine that has the Java Virtual Machine (JVM) installed. This makes Java platform-independent as the same code can run on Windows, Linux, macOS, etc., without any modification.

2. **Object-Oriented Programming (OOP)**: Java follows the principles of OOP, which include abstraction, encapsulation, inheritance, and polymorphism. This approach makes Java programs modular, reusable, and easier to maintain.
3. **Security**: Java provides a secure environment through features like the sandbox security model, which helps prevent unauthorized access to system resources. Additionally, Java offers bytecode verification, secure communication, and encryption APIs, making it ideal for internet-based applications.
4. **Automatic Memory Management (Garbage Collection)**: Java has an automatic garbage collector that manages memory, which reduces the need for manual memory management. This helps prevent memory leaks and improves program efficiency.
5. **Multithreading Support**: Java has built-in support for multithreading, enabling developers to write programs that can perform multiple tasks simultaneously. This makes Java a great choice for applications requiring real-time processing, such as gaming or multimedia applications.
6. **Rich API (Application Programming Interface)**: Java provides a vast set of libraries and frameworks that developers can use to quickly build applications. These libraries cover networking, input/output, data structures, user interface development, and more.
7. **Community Support and Open Source**: Java has a vast, active community, and being open-source, many libraries, tools, and frameworks are available for free, allowing developers to rapidly develop applications.

These features contribute to Java's popularity in building enterprise applications, mobile apps (Android), web applications, and more.

---

2. Explain the concept of the `main()` method in Java. Why is it essential for running a Java program?

Answer:
In Java, the `main()` method serves as the entry point for the program. It is the first method that the Java Virtual Machine (JVM) invokes when running a Java application. Without the `main()` method, the JVM will not know where to begin the execution of the program. The `main()` method has the following signature:

```
public static void main(String[] args)
```

1. **public**: The `main()` method is declared as `public` to make it accessible from outside the class, especially by the JVM. If the `main()` method was private, the JVM would not be able to access it, leading to an error.
2. **static**: The `main()` method is `static`, meaning it can be called without creating an instance of the class. This is important because, when the program starts, no objects have been created yet. By making `main()` static, we ensure that the method is accessible directly through the class.

3. **void**: The return type of the `main()` method is `void`, meaning it does not return any value. Since the purpose of the `main()` method is to start the program, there is no need for it to return any information.
4. **String[] args**: The `main()` method accepts a parameter of type `String[]`, which is an array of command-line arguments passed to the program. These arguments can be used to customize the behavior of the program based on user input or configuration files. For example, you might pass file paths, usernames, or other data that the program will process.

The `main()` method is essential because it sets the foundation for running any Java application. Once `main()` is called, you can invoke other methods, create objects, and execute your program's logic.

3. How does Java achieve platform independence? Explain the concept of bytecode and JVM.

Answer:
Java achieves platform independence through a combination of **bytecode** and the **Java Virtual Machine (JVM)**.

1. **Java Source Code**: Java programs are written in human-readable source code with the `.java` file extension. This code is platform-dependent at the source level.
2. **Compilation to Bytecode**: When a Java program is compiled, it is converted into an intermediate form called **bytecode**. Bytecode is a low-level, platform-neutral representation of the source code. It is stored in `.class` files, which contain instructions that are not specific to any particular computer architecture.
3. **Java Virtual Machine (JVM)**: The JVM is an abstraction layer that allows Java programs to run on any platform that has a compatible JVM implementation. The JVM takes the bytecode generated by the Java compiler and interprets or compiles it into machine-specific code for execution on the host machine.

The key point is that the **bytecode** is not tied to any operating system or hardware. As long as there is a JVM for a given platform (Windows, Linux, macOS, etc.), the same bytecode can be executed on all platforms without modification. This is what makes Java a **platform-independent** language—Java programs can be written once and run anywhere.

4. What is the difference between `int` and `Integer` in Java?

Answer:
The key difference between `int` and `Integer` in Java lies in the fact that `int` is a **primitive data type**, while `Integer` is a **wrapper class** that allows primitive data types to be used as objects. Here's a breakdown:

1. **`int` (Primitive Data Type)**:
   - o   `int` is a built-in, low-level data type that stores integer values directly in memory.
   - o   It is part of Java's basic data types and is not an object.
   - o   It occupies 4 bytes of memory.
   - o   `int` cannot be `null`. It always has a default value of 0 when declared as a field.
2. **`Integer` (Wrapper Class)**:
   - o   `Integer` is a class in the `java.lang` package that wraps an `int` value in an object.
   - o   It provides methods for converting between `int` and `String`, comparing values, and other utility functions.
   - o   It is used when an `int` value is needed in the context of objects, such as when using `Collections` (e.g., `ArrayList<Integer>`).
   - o   It can be `null` because it is an object, which is useful in situations where you may need to represent an absent or undefined value.

Example:

```
int num1 = 10;          // primitive type
Integer num2 = 20;      // wrapper class object
```

5. Explain the concept of object-oriented programming (OOP) in Java. How does Java implement OOP principles?

Answer:
Object-Oriented Programming (OOP) is a programming paradigm based on the concept of objects, which are instances of classes. Java is an object-oriented language that implements the following four fundamental principles of OOP:

1. **Encapsulation**:
   Encapsulation refers to the bundling of data (variables) and methods (functions) that operate on the data into a single unit called a **class**. It also involves restricting access to the internal workings of the class by using **access modifiers** like `private`, `protected`, and `public`. This ensures that the object's state is protected from unwanted access and modification.

   Example:

```
public class Person {
    private String name;   // private variable

    public String getName() {   // public getter method
        return name;
    }

    public void setName(String name) {   // public setter method
        this.name = name;
    }
}
```

2. **Inheritance**:
   Inheritance allows a class to inherit properties and methods from another class. The class that is inherited from is called the **superclass**, and the class that inherits is called the **subclass**. Inheritance promotes code reuse and makes it easier to extend existing functionality.

   Example:

```
public class Animal {
    public void eat() {
        System.out.println("Eating...");
    }
}

public class Dog extends Animal {
    public void bark() {
        System.out.println("Barking...");
    }
}
```

3. **Polymorphism**:
   Polymorphism means "many forms" and allows objects of different classes to be treated as objects of a common superclass. In Java, polymorphism can be achieved through **method overloading** (compile-time polymorphism) and **method overriding** (runtime polymorphism).

   Example (method overriding):

```
public class Animal {
    public void sound() {
        System.out.println("Some sound...");
    }
}

public class Dog extends Animal {
    @Override
    public void sound() {
        System.out.println("Barking...");
    }
}
```

4. **Abstraction**:
   Abstraction is the process of hiding the implementation details and showing only the essential features of an object. In Java, abstraction is achieved using **abstract classes** and **interfaces**. An abstract class can have abstract methods (without implementation) and concrete methods (with implementation). Interfaces allow a class to implement multiple behaviors by providing abstract methods that must be implemented by the class.

   Example:

```
public abstract class Animal {
```

```
        public abstract void sound();   // abstract method
    }
```

6. Describe the different types of loops available in Java with examples.

Answer:
Java provides several types of loops to execute a block of code multiple times based on conditions. The types of loops in Java are:

1. **For Loop**:
   The `for` loop is used when the number of iterations is known beforehand. It includes initialization, condition checking, and increment/decrement in a single statement.

   Example:

   ```java
   for (int i = 0; i < 5; i++) {
       System.out.println(i);
   }
   ```

2. **While Loop**:
   The `while` loop is used when the number of iterations is unknown and you want to repeat a block of code while a condition is true.

   Example:

   ```java
   int i = 0;
   while (i < 5) {
       System.out.println(i);
       i++;
   }
   ```

3. **Do-While Loop**:
   The `do-while` loop is similar to the `while` loop, but it guarantees that the block of code will be executed at least once, even if the condition is false initially.

   Example:

   ```java
   int i = 0;
   do {
       System.out.println(i);
       i++;
   } while (i < 5);
   ```

7. Explain the difference between method overloading and method overriding in Java.

Answer:
Method Overloading and **Method Overriding** are both techniques in Java used to define methods with the same name. However, they are different in their purpose and usage:

1. **Method Overloading**:
   Method overloading occurs when a class has multiple methods with the same name but different parameter lists (either by type, number, or both). Overloading is resolved at compile time (static polymorphism). The return type can also differ.

   Example:

```
class Display {
    public void show(int a) {
        System.out.println("Integer: " + a);
    }

    public void show(String a) {
        System.out.println("String: " + a);
    }
}
```

2. **Method Overriding**:
   Method overriding occurs when a subclass provides a specific implementation of a method that is already defined in its superclass. Overriding is resolved at runtime (dynamic polymorphism). The method signature must be the same as the superclass method.

   Example:

```
class Animal {
    public void sound() {
        System.out.println("Some sound...");
    }
}

class Dog extends Animal {
    @Override
    public void sound() {
        System.out.println("Barking...");
    }
}
```

8. What is the difference between == operator and `equals()` method in Java?

Answer:
In Java, the == operator and the `equals()` method are both used to compare objects, but they serve different purposes:

1. **== Operator**:
   The `==` operator compares the **memory addresses** (references) of two objects. This means it checks whether the two variables point to the exact same object in memory.

   Example:

   ```
   String str1 = new String("Hello");
   String str2 = new String("Hello");
   System.out.println(str1 == str2);   // false, different objects
   ```

2. **`equals()` Method**:
   The `equals()` method, which is defined in the `Object` class, is intended to compare the **content** of objects. For objects like `String`, `equals()` checks if the two objects have the same value, not the same reference.

   Example:

   ```
   System.out.println(str1.equals(str2));   // true, same content
   ```

---

9. Explain the concept of constructor in Java. What is the difference between a default constructor and a parameterized constructor?

Answer:
A **constructor** is a special method in Java that is called when an object is instantiated. It is used to initialize the object's state. Constructors have the same name as the class and do not have a return type.

1. **Default Constructor**:
   A default constructor is a no-argument constructor provided by Java if no other constructor is defined. It initializes object variables with default values (e.g., `null`, `0`, `false`).

   Example:

   ```java
   class Person {
       String name;
       int age;

       // Default constructor
       public Person() {
           name = "Unknown";
           age = 0;
       }
   }
   ```

2. **Parameterized Constructor**:
   A parameterized constructor is a constructor that accepts parameters to initialize the object's variables with specific values during object creation.

   Example:

```
class Person {
    String name;
    int age;

    // Parameterized constructor
    public Person(String name, int age) {
        this.name = name;
        this.age = age;
    }}
```

10. What are arrays in Java? How do you declare, initialize, and access elements in an array?

Answer:
In Java, an **array** is a collection of variables (elements) of the same data type, stored in a contiguous memory location. Arrays allow you to store multiple values in a single variable.

1. **Declaring an Array**: You declare an array by specifying the type of elements it will hold and the size of the array (or without size in case of dynamic arrays).

   Example:

```
int[] arr = new int[5];   // Declare an array of integers with size 5
```

2. **Initializing an Array**:
   You can initialize an array either at the time of declaration or later by assigning values to the elements.

   Example:

```
int[] arr = {1, 2, 3, 4, 5};   // Initialize the array with values
```

3. **Accessing Array Elements**:
   Array elements are accessed using an index. The index starts from 0 for the first element.

   Example:

```
System.out.println(arr[0]);   // Output: 1 (first element)
```

CHAPTER 2: CONTROL FLOW STATEMENTS

30 Multiple Choice Questions (MCQ)s:

---

1. Which of the following is NOT a control flow statement in Java?

a) if
b) for
c) void
d) switch

Answer: c) void

---

2. What is the output of the following code snippet?

```
int x = 10;
if (x > 5) {
    System.out.println("Greater");
} else {
    System.out.println("Smaller");
}
```

a) Greater
b) Smaller
c) Syntax Error
d) No output

Answer: a) Greater

---

3. What does the "else" block do in an "if-else" statement?

a) Executes if the condition is true
b) Executes if the condition is false
c) Never executes
d) Terminates the program

Answer: b) Executes if the condition is false

4. Which of the following is a valid use of the "switch" statement?

a) switch(5) { case 1: break; }
b) switch(5) { default: break; }
c) switch(5) { case 5: break; }
d) All of the above

Answer: d) All of the above

---

5. Which of the following is the correct syntax of a for loop?

a) for(int i = 0; i < 10; i++)
b) for(i = 0; i < 10; i++)
c) for(int i = 0; i < 10; i--)
d) for(int i = 10; i < 0; i++)

Answer: a) for(int i = 0; i < 10; i++)

---

6. What will the following code print?

```
int x = 3;
switch(x) {
    case 1:
        System.out.println("One");
        break;
    case 2:
        System.out.println("Two");
        break;
    case 3:
        System.out.println("Three");
        break;
    default:
        System.out.println("Default");
}
```

a) One
b) Two
c) Three
d) Default

Answer: c) Three

7. Which of the following statements is used to skip an iteration of a loop?

a) continue
b) break

c) exit
d) skip

Answer: a) continue

---

8. What is the output of the following code?

```
int i = 1;
while(i <= 5) {
    System.out.print(i + " ");
    i++;
}
```

a) 1 2 3 4 5
b) 1 2 3 4
c) Infinite loop
d) Error

Answer: a) 1 2 3 4 5

---

9. Which of the following is a valid syntax for the "if" statement?

a) if(x == 10) {
b) if x = 10 {
c) if x == 10;
d) if(10 == x)

Answer: a) if(x == 10) {

---

10. Which of the following operators is used in the condition of a switch case statement?

a) ==
b) =
c) !=
d) &&

Answer: a) ==

---

11. In a for loop, which part is executed first?

a) Initialization
b) Condition
c) Increment/Decrement
d) Block of code inside the loop

Answer: a) Initialization

12. What will be the output of the following code?

```
int x = 10;
if(x > 5) {
    System.out.println("Greater");
}
if(x == 10) {
    System.out.println("Equal");
}
```

a) Greater
b) Equal
c) Greater Equal
d) No output

Answer: c) Greater Equal

13. Which of the following statements is true for the "break" statement in a loop?

a) It stops the current iteration and moves to the next iteration
b) It terminates the loop entirely
c) It terminates the program
d) It executes only once per loop

Answer: b) It terminates the loop entirely

14. Which of the following is NOT a valid loop in Java?

a) for
b) while

c) do-while
d) until

Answer: d) until

---

15. What does the following code print?

```
int x = 4;
switch(x) {
    case 3:
        System.out.println("Three");
        break;
    case 4:
        System.out.println("Four");
        break;
    default:
        System.out.println("Default");
}
```

a) Three
b) Four
c) Default
d) Error

Answer: b) Four

---

16. What will the following code output?

```
int i = 0;
do {
    System.out.println(i);
    i++;
} while(i < 5);
```

a) 0 1 2 3 4
b) 1 2 3 4 5
c) 0 1 2 3
d) No output

Answer: a) 0 1 2 3 4

---

17. What will be the output of the following code?

```
int x = 10;
if(x < 5) {
    System.out.println("Smaller");
} else if(x == 10) {
    System.out.println("Equal to 10");
} else {
    System.out.println("Greater");
}
```

a) Smaller
b) Equal to 10
c) Greater
d) No output

Answer: b) Equal to 10

---

18. Which of the following is true about the "continue" statement?

a) It stops the loop completely
b) It skips the current iteration and moves to the next one
c) It terminates the program
d) It terminates the block of code

Answer: b) It skips the current iteration and moves to the next one

---

19. Which type of loop is guaranteed to execute at least once?

a) for
b) while
c) do-while
d) for-each

Answer: c) do-while

20. What will the following code print?

```
int x = 10;
if(x > 5) {
    if(x < 15) {
        System.out.println("Between 5 and 15");
    }
}
```

a) Between 5 and 15
b) No output
c) Error
d) Between 10 and 15

Answer: a) Between 5 and 15

---

21. How do you define the number of iterations in a for loop?

a) By the condition in the loop
b) By the number of elements in the array
c) By initializing the iterator variable
d) All of the above

Answer: d) All of the above

---

22. What will the following code print?

```
int i = 10;
while(i >= 0) {
    System.out.print(i + " ");
    i--;
}
```

a) 10 9 8 7 6 5 4 3 2 1 0
b) 9 8 7 6 5 4 3 2 1 0
c) Infinite loop
d) No output

Answer: a) 10 9 8 7 6 5 4 3 2 1 0

---

23. What is the syntax of a while loop?

a) while (condition) { statements }
b) while (statements) { condition }
c) while { statements (condition) }
d) while (condition) { }

Answer: a) while (condition) { statements }

---

24. What happens if the "break" statement is used inside a switch statement?

a) It breaks out of the entire program
b) It terminates the case block and exits the switch statement
c) It causes an infinite loop
d) It continues to the next case block

Answer: b) It terminates the case block and exits the switch statement

---

25. How many times will the following loop execute?

```
for(int i = 1; i <= 5; i++) {
    System.out.println(i);
}
```

a) 0
b) 5
c) 6
d) Infinite

Answer: b) 5

---

26. Which of the following is true about the switch statement in Java?

a) It can evaluate only integer values
b) It evaluates the condition in the case statements
c) It can evaluate multiple conditions using logical operators
d) It works with boolean values only

Answer: b) It evaluates the condition in the case statements

---

27. What will be the output of this code?

```
int x = 20;
if(x == 20) {
    System.out.println("Equal");
} else {
    System.out.println("Not equal");
}
```

a) Equal
b) Not equal
c) Error
d) No output

Answer: a) Equal

---

28. In Java, which of the following is used to create an infinite loop?

a) for(;;)
b) while(true)
c) do { } while(true);
d) All of the above

Answer: d) All of the above

---

29. Which of the following is the correct syntax for a do-while loop?

a) do { statement; } while(condition);
b) do while { statement; condition; }
c) do { statement; condition } until;
d) do (condition) { statement; }

Answer: a) do { statement; } while(condition);

---

30. What is the purpose of the default keyword in a switch case?

a) It ends the switch statement
b) It handles any value that does not match any case
c) It loops the program
d) It breaks out of a loop

Answer: b) It handles any value that does not match any case

30 short-length questions and answers :

1. What is a control flow statement in Java?

Answer: A control flow statement in Java allows the flow of execution to be altered based on certain conditions or loops, such as `if`, `else`, `switch`, `for`, `while`, and `do-while`.

2. What is the syntax of the `if` statement in Java?

Answer: The syntax is:

```
if (condition) {
    // code to be executed
}
```

3. What is the purpose of the `else` statement?

Answer: The `else` statement provides an alternative block of code to execute if the `if` condition is false.

4. What is the difference between `if` and `else if` in Java?

Answer: `if` is used to check the initial condition, while `else if` is used to check additional conditions when the previous `if` or `else if` conditions fail.

5. Explain the switch-case statement in Java.

Answer: The `switch` statement evaluates an expression and executes the corresponding `case` block if the value matches. It is an alternative to multiple `if-else` statements.

6. What will happen if no `break` statement is used in a `switch` case?

Answer: If no `break` is used, the program will "fall through" and continue executing the subsequent cases until a `break` is encountered or the switch statement ends.

7. What is the `break` statement used for in loops?

Answer: The `break` statement is used to exit a loop or switch statement immediately, regardless of the condition.

8. What is the use of the `continue` statement?

Answer: The `continue` statement skips the current iteration of a loop and proceeds with the next iteration.

9. What is the difference between `while` loop and `do-while` loop?

Answer: The `while` loop checks the condition before executing the code, while the `do-while` loop executes the code at least once before checking the condition.

10. What is the syntax for a `for` loop in Java?

Answer: The syntax is:

```
for(initialization; condition; increment/decrement) {
    // code to be executed
}
```

11. What is an infinite loop?

Answer: An infinite loop is a loop that never terminates, either because the condition is always true or the termination condition is never met.

12. What is the function of the `default` keyword in a switch statement?

Answer: The `default` keyword defines a block of code that is executed when none of the `case` values match the switch expression.

13. What is the difference between `for` loop and `while` loop?

Answer: The `for` loop is typically used when the number of iterations is known beforehand, whereas the `while` loop is used when the number of iterations is determined based on a condition.

14. What will the following code output?

```java
int i = 1;
while (i <= 5) {
    System.out.println(i);
    i++;
}
```

Answer: The output will be:
```
1 2 3 4 5
```

15. What is the result of the following switch statement?

```java
int x = 2;
switch (x) {
    case 1:
        System.out.println("One");
        break;
    case 2:
        System.out.println("Two");
        break;
    default:
        System.out.println("Default");
}
```

Answer: The output will be: `Two`

16. What is the purpose of using `else if` instead of multiple `if` statements?

Answer: `else if` allows checking multiple conditions sequentially, making the code more efficient by avoiding redundant checks.

17. Can you use a `switch` statement with boolean expressions in Java?

Answer: No, `switch` in Java only works with integral types (`byte`, `short`, `int`, `char`), enum, and `String`. It does not support boolean expressions.

18. How does the `do-while` loop differ from the `while` loop?

Answer: The `do-while` loop guarantees at least one execution of the loop body, whereas the `while` loop may not execute if the condition is false initially.

19. What does the `continue` statement do in a loop?

Answer: The `continue` statement skips the remaining code in the current iteration and proceeds to the next iteration of the loop.

20. What is the output of the following code?

```
int x = 5;
if (x > 3) {
    if (x < 10) {
        System.out.println("Between 3 and 10");
    }
}
```

Answer: The output will be: `Between 3 and 10`

21. What is the use of `break` in the `switch` statement?

Answer: The `break` statement is used to terminate the current case in the switch statement and prevent the execution of subsequent cases.

22. What happens if a `break` is omitted in a `switch` case?

Answer: If `break` is omitted, the program will "fall through" and execute all the subsequent case blocks until it encounters a `break` or the end of the `switch` block.

23. Can a `for` loop be used to iterate over an array in Java?

Answer: Yes, a `for` loop can be used to iterate over the elements of an array by using the array's index.

24. What is the output of the following code?

```
int x = 10;
switch (x) {
    case 5:
        System.out.println("Five");
        break;
    case 10:
        System.out.println("Ten");
        break;
    default:
        System.out.println("Other");
}
```

Answer: The output will be: Ten

25. What will the following code print?

```
int x = 0;
if (x == 0) {
    System.out.println("Zero");
} else {
    System.out.println("Not Zero");
}
```

Answer: The output will be: Zero

26. What is the syntax of the `for-each` loop in Java?

Answer: The syntax is:

```
for (type var : array) {
    // code to be executed
}
```

27. What is the purpose of the `if` statement in Java?

Answer: The `if` statement is used to execute a block of code only if a specified condition is true.

28. What is the result of using an uninitialized variable in a loop condition?

Answer: If a variable is not initialized before being used in a loop condition, it will cause a compile-time error.

---

29. What will the following code print?

```
int i = 1;
do {
    System.out.println(i);
    i++;
} while (i <= 3);
```

Answer: The output will be:
```
1 2 3
```

---

30. Can we use `continue` in a `switch` statement?

Answer: No, the `continue` statement cannot be used in a `switch` statement directly, but it can be used in loops inside the `switch` block.

15 practical questions with answers :

---

1. Write a program to check whether a number is positive, negative, or zero.

Answer:

```java
import java.util.Scanner;

public class CheckNumber {
    public static void main(String[] args) {
        Scanner sc = new Scanner(System.in);
        System.out.print("Enter a number: ");
        int num = sc.nextInt();

        if (num > 0) {
            System.out.println("The number is positive.");
        } else if (num < 0) {
            System.out.println("The number is negative.");
        } else {
            System.out.println("The number is zero.");
        }
    }
}
```

2. Write a program to find the largest of three numbers using `if-else` statement.

Answer:

```java
import java.util.Scanner;

public class LargestNumber {
    public static void main(String[] args) {
        Scanner sc = new Scanner(System.in);
        System.out.print("Enter three numbers: ");
        int a = sc.nextInt();
        int b = sc.nextInt();
        int c = sc.nextInt();

        if (a > b && a > c) {
            System.out.println(a + " is the largest number.");
        } else if (b > a && b > c) {
            System.out.println(b + " is the largest number.");
        } else {
            System.out.println(c + " is the largest number.");
        }
    }
}
```

3. Write a program to display the day of the week using `switch` statement.

Answer:

```java
import java.util.Scanner;

public class DayOfWeek {
    public static void main(String[] args) {
        Scanner sc = new Scanner(System.in);
        System.out.print("Enter a number (1-7): ");
        int day = sc.nextInt();

        switch (day) {
            case 1:
                System.out.println("Monday");
                break;
            case 2:
                System.out.println("Tuesday");
                break;
            case 3:
                System.out.println("Wednesday");
                break;
            case 4:
                System.out.println("Thursday");
                break;
            case 5:
                System.out.println("Friday");
                break;
            case 6:
```

```
            System.out.println("Saturday");
            break;
        case 7:
            System.out.println("Sunday");
            break;
        default:
            System.out.println("Invalid input!");
        }
    }
}
```

4. Write a program to check if a number is divisible by both 5 and 3.

Answer:

```java
import java.util.Scanner;

public class DivisibleBy5And3 {
    public static void main(String[] args) {
        Scanner sc = new Scanner(System.in);
        System.out.print("Enter a number: ");
        int num = sc.nextInt();

        if (num % 5 == 0 && num % 3 == 0) {
            System.out.println("The number is divisible by both 5 and 3.");
        } else {
            System.out.println("The number is not divisible by both 5 and
3.");
        }
    }
}
```

5. Write a program to print numbers from 1 to 10 using `for` loop.

Answer:

```java
public class PrintNumbers {
    public static void main(String[] args) {
        for (int i = 1; i <= 10; i++) {
            System.out.println(i);
        }
    }
}
```

6. Write a program to find the factorial of a number using `while` loop.

Answer:

```java
import java.util.Scanner;
```

```
public class Factorial {
    public static void main(String[] args) {
        Scanner sc = new Scanner(System.in);
        System.out.print("Enter a number: ");
        int num = sc.nextInt();
        int factorial = 1;

        while (num > 0) {
            factorial *= num;
            num--;
        }

        System.out.println("Factorial is: " + factorial);
    }
}
```

7. Write a program to print even numbers from 1 to 20 using `for` loop.

Answer:

```
public class EvenNumbers {
    public static void main(String[] args) {
        for (int i = 1; i <= 20; i++) {
            if (i % 2 == 0) {
                System.out.println(i);
            }
        }
    }
}
```

8. Write a program to find whether a number is prime or not.

Answer:

```
import java.util.Scanner;

public class PrimeNumber {
    public static void main(String[] args) {
        Scanner sc = new Scanner(System.in);
        System.out.print("Enter a number: ");
        int num = sc.nextInt();
        boolean isPrime = true;

        for (int i = 2; i <= num / 2; i++) {
            if (num % i == 0) {
                isPrime = false;
                break;
            }
        }

        if (isPrime) {
```

```java
            System.out.println(num + " is a prime number.");
        } else {
            System.out.println(num + " is not a prime number.");
        }
    }
}
```

9. Write a program to print the Fibonacci series up to the nth term.

Answer:

```java
import java.util.Scanner;

public class FibonacciSeries {
    public static void main(String[] args) {
        Scanner sc = new Scanner(System.in);
        System.out.print("Enter the number of terms: ");
        int n = sc.nextInt();

        int first = 0, second = 1;
        System.out.print("Fibonacci Series: " + first + " " + second);

        for (int i = 3; i <= n; i++) {
            int next = first + second;
            System.out.print(" " + next);
            first = second;
            second = next;
        }
    }
}
```

10. Write a program to count the number of digits in a number using `while` loop.

Answer:

```java
import java.util.Scanner;

public class CountDigits {
    public static void main(String[] args) {
        Scanner sc = new Scanner(System.in);
        System.out.print("Enter a number: ");
        int num = sc.nextInt();
        int count = 0;

        while (num != 0) {
            num /= 10;
            count++;
        }

        System.out.println("The number has " + count + " digits.");
    }
}
```

11. Write a program to find the sum of even numbers from 1 to 50 using `for` loop.

Answer:

```java
public class SumEvenNumbers {
    public static void main(String[] args) {
        int sum = 0;
        for (int i = 1; i <= 50; i++) {
            if (i % 2 == 0) {
                sum += i;
            }
        }
        System.out.println("Sum of even numbers from 1 to 50 is: " + sum);
    }
}
```

12. Write a program to print multiplication table of a given number.

Answer:

```java
import java.util.Scanner;

public class MultiplicationTable {
    public static void main(String[] args) {
        Scanner sc = new Scanner(System.in);
        System.out.print("Enter a number: ");
        int num = sc.nextInt();

        for (int i = 1; i <= 10; i++) {
            System.out.println(num + " * " + i + " = " + (num * i));
        }
    }
}
```

13. Write a program to print numbers from 1 to 10 using `do-while` loop.

Answer:

```java
public class PrintNumbersDoWhile {
    public static void main(String[] args) {
        int i = 1;
        do {
            System.out.println(i);
            i++;
        } while (i <= 10);
    }
}
```

14. Write a program to print the reverse of a given number.

Answer:

```java
import java.util.Scanner;

public class ReverseNumber {
    public static void main(String[] args) {
        Scanner sc = new Scanner(System.in);
        System.out.print("Enter a number: ");
        int num = sc.nextInt();
        int reverse = 0;

        while (num != 0) {
            reverse = reverse * 10 + num % 10;
            num /= 10;
        }

        System.out.println("Reversed number: " + reverse);
    }
}
```

15. Write a program to find the greatest common divisor (GCD) of two numbers using `while` loop.

Answer:

```java
import java.util.Scanner;

public class GCD {
    public static void main(String[] args) {
        Scanner sc = new Scanner(System.in);
        System.out.print("Enter two numbers: ");
        int a = sc.nextInt();
        int b = sc.nextInt();

        while (b != 0) {
            int temp = b;
            b = a % b;
            a = temp;
        }

        System.out.println("GCD is: " + a);
    }
}
```

10 long-length questions with answers:

1. Explain the use of `if-else` and `else-if` ladder in Java with an example.

Answer: The `if-else` and `else-if` ladder are decision-making constructs used in Java to execute specific blocks of code based on conditions.

- The `if` statement evaluates a condition, and if it's true, the block of code inside it is executed. If it's false, it moves to the `else` block, if present.
- The `else-if` ladder allows multiple conditions to be checked sequentially. The program moves through each `else-if` condition until one evaluates to `true`, and then the corresponding block of code is executed.

Example:

```java
import java.util.Scanner;

public class NumberClassification {
    public static void main(String[] args) {
        Scanner sc = new Scanner(System.in);
        System.out.print("Enter a number: ");
        int num = sc.nextInt();

        if (num > 0) {
            System.out.println("The number is positive.");
        } else if (num < 0) {
            System.out.println("The number is negative.");
        } else {
            System.out.println("The number is zero.");
        }
    }
}
```

In this example, based on the input, the program checks whether the number is positive, negative, or zero.

---

2. What is the difference between `while`, `do-while`, and `for` loops in Java? Provide examples.

Answer: The three loops in Java serve the purpose of iterating over a block of code multiple times but differ in their structure and the point where the condition is checked.

- **`while` loop**: The condition is checked before the execution of the block of code. If the condition is false initially, the loop will not execute at all.

  Example:

  ```java
  int i = 1;
  while (i <= 5) {
  ```

```
        System.out.println(i);
        i++;
    }
```

- **do-while loop**: The condition is checked after the block of code is executed. This guarantees that the block will execute at least once, even if the condition is false.

  Example:

```
int i = 1;
do {
    System.out.println(i);
    i++;
} while (i <= 5);
```

- **for loop**: It is often used when the number of iterations is known. It includes the initialization, condition, and iteration statement in one line.

  Example:

```
for (int i = 1; i <= 5; i++) {
    System.out.println(i);
}
```

The while loop checks the condition first, the do-while loop guarantees one execution, and the for loop is compact and often used for counting or iterating a known number of times.

---

3. Explain the use of switch statement in Java with an example. How does it differ from if-else?

Answer: The switch statement in Java allows you to evaluate a single expression against multiple case labels and execute the corresponding block of code. It is often used when there are multiple conditions based on a single variable.

- The switch statement is more efficient than multiple if-else conditions when there are several conditions to check for a single variable.
- It compares the value of the expression with the case labels and executes the corresponding block.

Example:

```
import java.util.Scanner;

public class DayOfWeek {
    public static void main(String[] args) {
        Scanner sc = new Scanner(System.in);
        System.out.print("Enter a day number (1-7): ");
```

```
    int day = sc.nextInt();

    switch (day) {
        case 1: System.out.println("Monday"); break;
        case 2: System.out.println("Tuesday"); break;
        case 3: System.out.println("Wednesday"); break;
        case 4: System.out.println("Thursday"); break;
        case 5: System.out.println("Friday"); break;
        case 6: System.out.println("Saturday"); break;
        case 7: System.out.println("Sunday"); break;
        default: System.out.println("Invalid day");
    }
  }
}
```

Difference from `if-else`:

- `switch` is faster when you have multiple conditions checking the same variable.
- `if-else` is better suited for checking ranges or conditions that are not based on discrete values.

4. What is the `break` statement used for in loops and switch-case statements? Provide examples.

Answer: The `break` statement in Java is used to terminate a loop or a `switch` statement prematurely. When the `break` statement is encountered, the control exits from the loop or the `switch` block immediately, and the next statement after the loop or `switch` is executed.

- **In loops**: The `break` statement can be used to exit the loop early based on a certain condition.

  Example:

  ```
  for (int i = 1; i <= 10; i++) {
      if (i == 5) {
          break;  // Exits the loop when i is 5
      }
      System.out.println(i);
  }
  ```

- **In `switch-case`**: The `break` statement is used to terminate the execution of the `switch` case and prevent the fall-through to other cases.

  Example:

  ```
  int day = 3;

  switch (day) {
  ```

```
    case 1: System.out.println("Monday"); break;
    case 2: System.out.println("Tuesday"); break;
    case 3: System.out.println("Wednesday"); break;   // This will
execute
    default: System.out.println("Invalid day");
}
```

5. What is the `continue` statement in Java and how does it differ from `break`? Provide examples.

Answer: The `continue` statement is used inside loops to skip the current iteration and continue with the next iteration of the loop. Unlike `break`, which exits the loop, `continue` simply skips the current iteration and moves to the next one.

Example:

```
for (int i = 1; i <= 5; i++) {
    if (i == 3) {
        continue;   // Skips printing 3
    }
    System.out.println(i);
}
```

Output:

```
1
2
4
5
```

Difference from `break`:

- `break` exits the entire loop or `switch` statement.
- `continue` skips only the current iteration of the loop and moves to the next one.

6. Explain how `nested if-else` works with an example in Java.

Answer: A nested `if-else` is an `if` statement inside another `if` statement. This allows you to make more complex decisions where each condition depends on a prior condition being true.

Example:

```
import java.util.Scanner;

public class NestedIfExample {
    public static void main(String[] args) {
```

```
Scanner sc = new Scanner(System.in);
System.out.print("Enter your age: ");
int age = sc.nextInt();

if (age >= 18) {
    if (age < 65) {
        System.out.println("You are an adult.");
    } else {
        System.out.println("You are a senior citizen.");
    }
} else {
    System.out.println("You are a minor.");
}
}
}
```

In this example, the first condition checks if the person is an adult, and if so, it checks if they are a senior citizen or not.

---

7. How does the `for` loop work with multiple conditions in Java? Provide an example where multiple conditions are checked in a `for` loop.

Answer: In Java, the `for` loop allows you to define multiple conditions in the initialization, condition, and iteration sections. Multiple conditions can be used in the `for` loop by combining them using logical operators like `&&` (AND) or `||` (OR).

Example:

```
public class ForLoopExample {
    public static void main(String[] args) {
        for (int i = 1, j = 10; i <= 5 && j >= 6; i++, j--) {
            System.out.println("i = " + i + ", j = " + j);
        }    }}
```

In this example, the `for` loop runs as long as both conditions `i <= 5` and `j >= 6` are true, and `i` increments while `j` decrements in each iteration.

---

8. What is the importance of the `default` case in a `switch` statement? Explain with an example.

Answer: The `default` case in a `switch` statement is used when none of the `case` labels match the value of the expression being evaluated. It acts as a fallback option. It is not mandatory to include the `default` case, but it is good practice to provide it to handle unexpected or invalid input.

Example:

```
import java.util.Scanner;

public class SwitchExample {
    public static void main(String[] args) {
        Scanner sc = new Scanner(System.in);
        System.out.print("Enter a day number (1-7): ");
        int day = sc.nextInt();

        switch (day) {
            case 1: System.out.println("Monday"); break;
            case 2: System.out.println("Tuesday"); break;
            case 3: System.out.println("Wednesday"); break;
            case 4: System.out.println("Thursday"); break;
            case 5: System.out.println("Friday"); break;
            case 6: System.out.println("Saturday"); break;
            case 7: System.out.println("Sunday"); break;
            default: System.out.println("Invalid input. Please enter a number
between 1 and 7.");
        }
    }
}
```

Here, if the user enters an invalid number, the `default` case will handle it by providing an appropriate message.

---

9. What are the advantages and limitations of using `switch` over `if-else`?

Answer: **Advantages of `switch`:**

- **Efficiency**: For checking multiple conditions on a single variable, `switch` can be more efficient than a series of `if-else` statements.
- **Readability**: It provides a cleaner, more readable structure when there are many conditions checking the same variable.
- **Performance**: For large numbers of cases, `switch` statements can sometimes be faster due to the way they are compiled.

Limitations of `switch`:

- **Limited condition types**: A `switch` statement can only be used with variables that are of a specific type such as `int`, `char`, `String`, or `enum`. It cannot be used with ranges or complex expressions.
- **No condition expressions**: `switch` only compares the expression against fixed `case` values, unlike `if-else`, which can handle complex boolean expressions.

10. Describe how the `if` statement works with logical operators like `&&` and `||`. Provide examples.

Answer: The `if` statement can combine multiple conditions using logical operators. The most common logical operators in Java are:

- **`&&` (AND)**: The condition evaluates to `true` only if both operands are `true`.
- **`||` (OR)**: The condition evaluates to `true` if at least one operand is `true`.

Examples:

- **Using `&&`:**

```
int age = 25;
int salary = 30000;

if (age > 18 && salary > 25000) {
    System.out.println("Eligible for the loan.");
} else {
    System.out.println("Not eligible for the loan.");
}
```

- **Using `||`:**

```
int age = 16;
boolean hasPermission = true;

if (age >= 18 || hasPermission) {
    System.out.println("Allowed to watch the movie.");
} else {
    System.out.println("Not allowed to watch the movie.");
}
```

In these examples, the `if` statement checks conditions with logical operators to determine the result based on both conditions being `true` or at least one condition being `true`.

CHAPTER 3: OBJECT-ORIENTED PROGRAMMING (OOP) CONCEPTS

30 multiple-choice questions (MCQs)::

1. What is the key principle of Object-Oriented Programming?

a) Functions
b) Objects
c) Logic
d) Data structures
Answer: b) Objects

2. Which of the following is not an OOP principle?

a) Abstraction
b) Encapsulation
c) Inheritance
d) Compilation
Answer: d) Compilation

3. Which of the following is used to hide the internal details of an object?

a) Inheritance
b) Polymorphism
c) Abstraction
d) Encapsulation
Answer: c) Abstraction

4. What is the main benefit of using Encapsulation in Java?

a) Increased performance
b) Data hiding
c) Better memory management
d) Faster execution
Answer: b) Data hiding

5. Which of the following is a feature of Java that supports OOP?

a) Functions
b) Interfaces
c) Pointers
d) None of the above
Answer: b) Interfaces

6. What is inheritance in Java?

a) A way to share variables and methods across different classes
b) A way to restrict access to class members
c) A way to implement the multiple inheritances
d) A way to hide methods from other classes
Answer: a) A way to share variables and methods across different classes

7. Which keyword is used to create a subclass in Java?

a) super
b) this
c) extends
d) implements
Answer: c) extends

8. Which of the following statements is true about the `super` keyword?

a) It is used to call a parent class constructor
b) It is used to call a child class constructor
c) It is used to access private variables
d) It is used to override a method
Answer: a) It is used to call a parent class constructor

9. Which of the following is an example of Polymorphism in Java?

a) Method Overloading
b) Method Overriding
c) Both a and b
d) None of the above
Answer: c) Both a and b

10. Which of the following terms is used to refer to a function in a class in Java?

a) Method
b) Constructor
c) Interface
d) Object
Answer: a) Method

11. What is the purpose of the `abstract` class in Java?

a) To provide a base class with partial implementation
b) To define an interface
c) To allow inheritance
d) To ensure multiple class inheritance
Answer: a) To provide a base class with partial implementation

12. Which of the following is the correct syntax for declaring an abstract method in Java?

a) `abstract void myMethod();`
b) `void abstract myMethod();`
c) `abstract void MyMethod;`
d) `void abstract myMethod();`
Answer: a) `abstract void myMethod();`

13. Which of the following is an example of method overloading?

a) A method with the same name but different return type
b) A method with the same name but different parameters
c) A method with different names
d) A method that is private
Answer: b) A method with the same name but different parameters

14. What does the term "constructor" refer to in Java?

a) A special method used to initialize objects
b) A method that deletes objects
c) A method that creates variables
d) A method that is invoked at the start of the program
Answer: a) A special method used to initialize objects

15. Which of the following can be a constructor in Java?

a) A method that returns a value
b) A method with the same name as the class
c) A method with no parameters
d) A static method
Answer: b) A method with the same name as the class

16. What is a class in Java?

a) A blueprint for creating objects
b) A variable
c) A method for running the program
d) A data type
Answer: a) A blueprint for creating objects

17. What does the `this` keyword refer to in Java?

a) The current object
b) The parent class

c) A static variable
d) An abstract method
Answer: a) The current object

18. Which of the following is true about method overriding in Java?

a) Method overriding is related to the concept of Polymorphism
b) The method in the subclass must have the same name, return type, and parameters as the method in the parent class
c) Both a and b
d) None of the above
Answer: c) Both a and b

19. Which of the following is used to achieve multiple inheritance in Java?

a) Interfaces
b) Abstract classes
c) Constructors
d) None of the above
Answer: a) Interfaces

20. What is an interface in Java?

a) A class with a constructor
b) A class without implementation of methods
c) A class with all methods defined
d) A class that extends another class
Answer: b) A class without implementation of methods

21. How can you prevent a class from being subclassed in Java?

a) Use the `final` keyword before the class declaration
b) Use the `private` keyword
c) Use the `abstract` keyword
d) Use the `static` keyword
Answer: a) Use the `final` keyword before the class declaration

22. Which of the following is true about the `final` keyword in Java?

a) It can be used with methods to prevent them from being overridden
b) It can be used with variables to make them constants
c) It can be used with classes to prevent inheritance
d) All of the above
Answer: d) All of the above

23. What does the `instanceof` operator do in Java?

a) Checks if an object is an instance of a given class or subclass
b) Creates an instance of a class
c) Creates an object
d) None of the above
Answer: a) Checks if an object is an instance of a given class or subclass

24. What is method hiding in Java?

a) A subclass method with the same signature as the superclass method
b) A method in the parent class that cannot be called
c) A method with the same name but different parameters in the same class
d) A method in the child class that overrides the parent method
Answer: a) A subclass method with the same signature as the superclass method

25. Which of the following is correct about constructors in Java?

a) A constructor can have a return type
b) A constructor is invoked using the `new` keyword
c) A constructor can be inherited
d) A constructor cannot be overloaded
Answer: b) A constructor is invoked using the `new` keyword

26. Which of the following statements about inheritance is correct?

a) A subclass can inherit from multiple classes
b) A subclass can inherit from one class only
c) A subclass cannot override methods from the superclass
d) A subclass can inherit private methods from the superclass
Answer: b) A subclass can inherit from one class only

27. Which keyword in Java is used to refer to the superclass of the current object?

a) super
b) this
c) parent
d) current
Answer: a) super

28. Which of the following is true for a `final` method in Java?

a) It cannot be overridden in any subclass
b) It can be overridden in a subclass

c) It can be used only in abstract classes
d) It cannot be called in a subclass
Answer: a) It cannot be overridden in any subclass

29. Which of the following is true about the `Object` class in Java?

a) Every class in Java inherits from the `Object` class
b) The `Object` class is only used for object comparison
c) `Object` class is only used for creating objects
d) None of the above
Answer: a) Every class in Java inherits from the `Object` class

30. What is the result of the following code?

```
class Animal {
    void sound() {
        System.out.println("Animal sound");
    }
}
class Dog extends Animal {
    void sound() {
        System.out.println("Bark");
    }
}
public class Test {
    public static void main(String[] args) {
        Animal a = new Dog();
        a.sound();
    }
}
```

a) Animal sound
b) Bark
c) Compilation error
d) Runtime exception
Answer: b) Bark

30 short questions with answers:

1. What is Object-Oriented Programming (OOP)?

Answer: OOP is a programming paradigm based on the concept of "objects," which contain both data and methods that operate on the data.

2. What are the four main principles of OOP?

Answer: The four main principles of OOP are Abstraction, Encapsulation, Inheritance, and Polymorphism.

3. What is a class in Java?

Answer: A class in Java is a blueprint or template for creating objects. It defines the properties and behaviors (fields and methods) of objects.

4. What is an object in Java?

Answer: An object is an instance of a class. It contains the actual values for the properties defined by the class and can invoke methods.

5. What is Abstraction in OOP?

Answer: Abstraction is the process of hiding the implementation details and showing only the functionality to the user.

6. What is Encapsulation in OOP?

Answer: Encapsulation is the technique of wrapping data (variables) and methods that operate on the data into a single unit or class, and restricting access to the data.

7. What is Inheritance in OOP?

Answer: Inheritance is the mechanism by which one class can inherit properties and behaviors (fields and methods) from another class.

8. What is Polymorphism in OOP?

Answer: Polymorphism is the ability of one method, operator, or object to behave in multiple forms. It allows the same method to behave differently based on the object it is acting upon.

9. What is a constructor in Java?

Answer: A constructor is a special method in a class that is used to initialize objects when they are created.

10. What is method overloading?

Answer: Method overloading is when multiple methods have the same name but differ in the number or type of their parameters.

11. What is method overriding?

Answer: Method overriding occurs when a subclass provides a specific implementation for a method that is already defined in its superclass.

12. What is the difference between method overloading and method overriding?

Answer: Method overloading involves creating multiple methods with the same name but different parameters, while method overriding is when a subclass defines a method with the same signature as in the parent class to modify its behavior.

13. What is the 'super' keyword in Java?

Answer: The `super` keyword refers to the superclass (parent class) of the current object. It is used to access superclass methods and constructors.

14. What is the 'this' keyword in Java?

Answer: The `this` keyword refers to the current object within a class. It is used to distinguish between instance variables and parameters with the same name.

15. What is an abstract class in Java?

Answer: An abstract class in Java is a class that cannot be instantiated and may contain abstract methods that must be implemented by subclasses.

16. What is an interface in Java?

Answer: An interface in Java is a reference type that defines a contract for classes to follow. It contains only abstract methods and constants.

17. What is the difference between an abstract class and an interface?

Answer: An abstract class can contain both abstract and non-abstract methods, while an interface can only contain abstract methods and constants.

18. What is a default constructor?

Answer: A default constructor is a constructor that is automatically provided by Java if no constructor is explicitly defined. It has no parameters.

19. What does the 'final' keyword do in Java?

Answer: The `final` keyword is used to define constants, prevent method overriding, and prevent class inheritance.

20. Can a constructor be overloaded?

Answer: Yes, constructors can be overloaded by providing different parameter lists.

21. What is the difference between 'final', 'finally', and 'finalize' in Java?

Answer: `final` is used for constants, methods, and classes; `finally` is used for blocks that execute after try-catch; `finalize` is a method that is called before an object is garbage collected.

22. What is multiple inheritance and how is it supported in Java?

Answer: Java does not support multiple inheritance through classes, but it can be achieved using interfaces.

23. What is a static method in Java?

Answer: A static method belongs to the class rather than an instance of the class and can be called without creating an object of the class.

24. What is the 'instanceof' keyword in Java?

Answer: The `instanceof` keyword is used to check whether an object is an instance of a particular class or subclass.

25. What is the purpose of the 'protected' access modifier in Java?

Answer: The `protected` access modifier allows access to members of a class from within the same package or subclasses.

26. What is the difference between 'public' and 'private' access modifiers?

Answer: `public` allows access from any class, while `private` restricts access to the members of the class in which they are defined.

27. What is the difference between 'static' and 'non-static' members?

Answer: Static members belong to the class and can be accessed without an instance, while non-static members belong to an instance of the class and require an object to be accessed.

28. Can an interface extend another interface?

Answer: Yes, an interface can extend another interface, allowing it to inherit the abstract methods of the parent interface.

29. What is constructor chaining in Java?

Answer: Constructor chaining refers to the process where one constructor calls another constructor of the same class or the superclass.

30. What is the role of a superclass and subclass in inheritance?

Answer: A superclass is a class that provides common properties and behaviors to its subclasses. A subclass inherits methods and fields from the superclass and can also add its own functionality.

These short questions and answers cover the essential concepts of OOP in Java, helping beginners understand the foundational principles of Object-Oriented Programming.

12 practical questions with:

1. Write a Java program to define a class `Person` with fields `name` and `age`, and a method to display the details of a person. Create an object of `Person` and call the display method.

Answer:

```java
class Person {
    String name;
    int age;

    // Constructor to initialize the fields
    Person(String name, int age) {
        this.name = name;
        this.age = age;
    }

    // Method to display details
    void displayDetails() {
        System.out.println("Name: " + name);
        System.out.println("Age: " + age);
    }

    public static void main(String[] args) {
        // Creating an object of Person class
        Person person1 = new Person("Alice", 25);
        person1.displayDetails();
    }
}
```

2. Write a Java program to implement method overloading by creating multiple `add()` methods that can add two integers, three integers, or two floating-point numbers.

Answer:

```java
class Calculator {
    // Method to add two integers
    int add(int a, int b) {
        return a + b;
```

```
    }

    // Method to add three integers
    int add(int a, int b, int c) {
        return a + b + c;
    }

    // Method to add two floating-point numbers
    double add(double a, double b) {
        return a + b;
    }

    public static void main(String[] args) {
        Calculator calc = new Calculator();
        System.out.println("Sum of 5 and 10: " + calc.add(5, 10));
        System.out.println("Sum of 1, 2 and 3: " + calc.add(1, 2, 3));
        System.out.println("Sum of 5.5 and 4.5: " + calc.add(5.5, 4.5));
    }
}
```

3. Write a Java program to demonstrate method overriding by creating a superclass Animal and a subclass Dog that overrides the makeSound() method.

Answer:

```
class Animal {
    void makeSound() {
        System.out.println("Animal makes a sound");
    }
}

class Dog extends Animal {
    @Override
    void makeSound() {
        System.out.println("Dog barks");
    }

    public static void main(String[] args) {
        Animal animal = new Animal();
        animal.makeSound();

        Dog dog = new Dog();
        dog.makeSound(); // Method overriding in action
    }
}
```

4. Write a Java program to create an abstract class Shape with an abstract method draw(). Create subclasses Circle and Rectangle that implement the draw() method.

Answer:

```
abstract class Shape {
```

```
    abstract void draw();
}

class Circle extends Shape {
    @Override
    void draw() {
        System.out.println("Drawing Circle");
    }
}

class Rectangle extends Shape {
    @Override
    void draw() {
        System.out.println("Drawing Rectangle");
    }
}

public class Main {
    public static void main(String[] args) {
        Shape shape1 = new Circle();
        shape1.draw(); // Circle's draw method

        Shape shape2 = new Rectangle();
        shape2.draw(); // Rectangle's draw method
    }
}
```

5. Write a Java program that demonstrates the use of the `super` keyword to access a superclass method from a subclass.

Answer:

```
class Animal {
    void sound() {
        System.out.println("Animal makes a sound");
    }
}

class Dog extends Animal {
    void sound() {
        System.out.println("Dog barks");
        super.sound(); // Calling superclass method
    }

    public static void main(String[] args) {
        Dog dog = new Dog();
        dog.sound();
    }
}
```

6. Write a Java program that uses the `this` keyword to differentiate between instance variables and parameters when both have the same name.

Answer:

```java
class Person {
    String name;

    // Constructor with parameters
    Person(String name) {
        this.name = name; // 'this' differentiates the instance variable from
the parameter
    }

    void display() {
        System.out.println("Name: " + name);
    }

    public static void main(String[] args) {
        Person person = new Person("Alice");
        person.display();
    }
}
```

7. Write a Java program to demonstrate the concept of constructor chaining by calling one constructor from another constructor within the same class.

Answer:

```java
class Person {
    String name;
    int age;

    // Constructor with two parameters
    Person(String name, int age) {
        this.name = name;
        this.age = age;
    }

    // Constructor with one parameter, calling the two-parameter constructor
    Person(String name) {
        this(name, 25); // Constructor chaining
    }

    void display() {
        System.out.println("Name: " + name);
        System.out.println("Age: " + age);
    }

    public static void main(String[] args) {
        Person person = new Person("Alice");
        person.display(); // Age defaults to 25
    }
}
```

8. Write a Java program to demonstrate the use of the `instanceof` operator.

Answer:

```
class Animal {}

class Dog extends Animal {}

public class Test {
    public static void main(String[] args) {
        Animal animal = new Dog();

        if (animal instanceof Dog) {
            System.out.println("animal is an instance of Dog");
        }

        if (animal instanceof Animal) {
            System.out.println("animal is an instance of Animal");
        }
    }
}
```

9. Write a Java program to create a class `Student` with a method `calculateGrade()` that uses `if-else` conditions to assign a grade based on marks.

Answer:

```
class Student {
    int marks;

    // Constructor
    Student(int marks) {
        this.marks = marks;
    }

    void calculateGrade() {
        if (marks >= 90) {
            System.out.println("Grade: A");
        } else if (marks >= 75) {
            System.out.println("Grade: B");
        } else if (marks >= 60) {
            System.out.println("Grade: C");
        } else {
            System.out.println("Grade: D");
        }
    }

    public static void main(String[] args) {
        Student student = new Student(85);
        student.calculateGrade();
    }
}
```

10. Write a Java program to implement a `Person` class with `private` fields and provide getter and setter methods to access and modify these fields.

Answer:

```java
class Person {
    private String name;
    private int age;

    // Getter method for name
    public String getName() {
        return name;
    }

    // Setter method for name
    public void setName(String name) {
        this.name = name;
    }

    // Getter method for age
    public int getAge() {
        return age;
    }

    // Setter method for age
    public void setAge(int age) {
        this.age = age;
    }

    public static void main(String[] args) {
        Person person = new Person();
        person.setName("Alice");
        person.setAge(30);

        System.out.println("Name: " + person.getName());
        System.out.println("Age: " + person.getAge());
    }
}
```

11. Write a Java program to demonstrate polymorphism by creating a superclass Shape and two subclasses Circle and Square that have different implementations of a method area().

Answer:

```java
class Shape {
    // Method to calculate area (to be overridden)
    double area() {
        return 0;
    }
}

class Circle extends Shape {
    double radius;

    Circle(double radius) {
        this.radius = radius;
    }

    @Override
```

```java
    double area() {
        return Math.PI * radius * radius;
    }
}

class Square extends Shape {
    double side;

    Square(double side) {
        this.side = side;
    }

    @Override
    double area() {
        return side * side;
    }
}

public class Test {
    public static void main(String[] args) {
        Shape shape1 = new Circle(5);
        Shape shape2 = new Square(4);

        System.out.println("Area of Circle: " + shape1.area());
        System.out.println("Area of Square: " + shape2.area());
    }
}
```

12. Write a Java program to implement an interface `Vehicle` with a method `start()`, and implement this interface in two classes `Car` and `Bike`.

Answer:

```java
interface Vehicle {
    void start();
}

class Car implements Vehicle {
    public void start() {
        System.out.println("Car started");
    }
}

class Bike implements Vehicle {
    public void start() {
        System.out.println("Bike started");
    }
}

public class Main {
    public static void main(String[] args) {
        Vehicle car = new Car();
        car.start(); // Car started

        Vehicle bike = new Bike();
```

```
        bike.start(); // Bike started
    }
}
```

Concepts in Java:

1. Explain the four fundamental concepts of Object-Oriented Programming (OOP) in Java with examples.

Answer:

The four fundamental concepts of OOP are:

1. **Encapsulation**: Encapsulation is the concept of bundling the data (variables) and methods (functions) that operate on the data into a single unit known as a class. It helps in hiding the internal workings of an object and provides access to the data via public methods (getters and setters).

    Example:

    ```
    class Person {
        private String name;
        private int age;

        // Getter method
        public String getName() {
            return name;
        }

        // Setter method
        public void setName(String name) {
            this.name = name;
        }

        public void displayDetails() {
            System.out.println("Name: " + name);
            System.out.println("Age: " + age);
        }
    }
    ```

2. **Abstraction**: Abstraction is the process of hiding the complex implementation details and showing only the necessary functionalities. In Java, abstraction is achieved through abstract classes and interfaces.

    Example:

    ```
    abstract class Animal {
        abstract void makeSound();
    }
    ```

```
class Dog extends Animal {
    void makeSound() {
        System.out.println("Bark");
    }
}
```

3. **Inheritance**: Inheritance allows a class to inherit the properties and behaviors (methods) of another class. It enables code reuse and the creation of hierarchical relationships between classes.

   Example:

```
class Animal {
    void eat() {
        System.out.println("Eating...");
    }
}

class Dog extends Animal {
    void bark() {
        System.out.println("Barking...");
    }
}
```

4. **Polymorphism**: Polymorphism means the ability to take many forms. In Java, polymorphism allows one interface to be used for different data types, mainly achieved through method overriding and method overloading.

   Example:

```
class Animal {
    void makeSound() {
        System.out.println("Animal makes sound");
    }
}

class Dog extends Animal {
    @Override
    void makeSound() {
        System.out.println("Dog barks");
    }
}
```

2. What is method overloading in Java? Explain with an example.

Answer:

Method overloading in Java is a feature that allows a class to have more than one method having the same name, but the methods must have different parameters (either different number of parameters or different types of parameters).

Overloading helps to perform similar tasks in different ways, based on the number or types of arguments passed.

Example:

```
class Calculator {
    // Overloaded method to add two integers
    int add(int a, int b) {
        return a + b;
    }

    // Overloaded method to add three integers
    int add(int a, int b, int c) {
        return a + b + c;
    }

    // Overloaded method to add two double values
    double add(double a, double b) {
        return a + b;
    }

    public static void main(String[] args) {
        Calculator calc = new Calculator();
        System.out.println("Sum of 5 and 10: " + calc.add(5, 10));
        System.out.println("Sum of 1, 2, and 3: " + calc.add(1, 2, 3));
        System.out.println("Sum of 1.5 and 2.5: " + calc.add(1.5, 2.5));
    }
}
```

In this example, the `add()` method is overloaded with different signatures to handle both integer and floating-point numbers.

3. Explain method overriding in Java with a real-world example.

Answer:

Method overriding occurs when a subclass provides a specific implementation for a method that is already defined in its superclass. The overridden method in the subclass must have the same signature (name, return type, and parameters) as the method in the superclass.

Overriding allows a subclass to provide its own version of a method while keeping the method signature consistent across classes.

Example:

```
class Animal {
    void sound() {
        System.out.println("Animal makes a sound");
    }
}

class Dog extends Animal {
```

```
        @Override
        void sound() {
            System.out.println("Dog barks");
        }
}

class Main {
    public static void main(String[] args) {
        Animal myDog = new Dog();
        myDog.sound();   // Output: Dog barks
    }
}
```

In this example, `sound()` is overridden in the `Dog` class to provide its specific implementation, replacing the generic sound defined in the `Animal` class.

4. What is an abstract class? How is it different from an interface?

Answer:

An **abstract class** is a class that cannot be instantiated on its own and may contain abstract methods (methods without implementation) that must be implemented by subclasses.

- **Abstract class:**
  - Can have both abstract (without implementation) and concrete (with implementation) methods.
  - Can have instance variables.
  - A class can inherit only one abstract class (single inheritance).
- **Interface:**
  - Can only have abstract methods (prior to Java 8), and from Java 8 onwards, it can have default and static methods with implementations.
  - Cannot have instance variables (can only have constants).
  - A class can implement multiple interfaces (multiple inheritance).

Example:

```
// Abstract Class
abstract class Animal {
    abstract void sound(); // abstract method

    void eat() { // concrete method
        System.out.println("Eating");
    }
}

// Interface
interface Vehicle {
    void drive(); // abstract method
}

class Dog extends Animal {
```

```
    @Override
    void sound() {
        System.out.println("Barks");
    }
}

class Car implements Vehicle {
    @Override
    public void drive() {
        System.out.println("Driving car");
    }
}
```

5. Explain the concept of constructor overloading in Java with an example.

Answer:

Constructor overloading in Java allows a class to have more than one constructor, each with different parameters. This is useful when you want to initialize an object in different ways.

Constructor overloading is similar to method overloading but applies to constructors.

Example:

```
class Person {
    String name;
    int age;

    // Constructor with one parameter
    Person(String name) {
        this.name = name;
        this.age = 0; // Default age
    }

    // Constructor with two parameters
    Person(String name, int age) {
        this.name = name;
        this.age = age;
    }

    void displayDetails() {
        System.out.println("Name: " + name);
        System.out.println("Age: " + age);
    }

    public static void main(String[] args) {
        Person person1 = new Person("Alice");
        Person person2 = new Person("Bob", 30);
        person1.displayDetails();
        person2.displayDetails();
    }
}
```

In this example, the class `Person` has two constructors that are overloaded to allow object initialization with different sets of parameters.

6. What is polymorphism in Java? Explain the types of polymorphism with examples.

Answer:

Polymorphism is the ability of an object to take many forms. In Java, polymorphism allows one interface to be used for different types of objects. It is primarily classified into two types:

1. **Compile-time polymorphism** (Method Overloading): This occurs when the method is overloaded with different parameters.

   Example:

```
class Calculator {
    int add(int a, int b) {
        return a + b;
    }

    double add(double a, double b) {
        return a + b;
    }
}
```

2. **Runtime polymorphism** (Method Overriding): This occurs when a subclass provides a specific implementation for a method that is already defined in its superclass.

   Example:

```
class Animal {
    void sound() {
        System.out.println("Animal makes sound");
    }
}

class Dog extends Animal {
    @Override
    void sound() {
        System.out.println("Dog barks");
    }
}

class Main {
    public static void main(String[] args) {
        Animal animal = new Dog();
        animal.sound();   // Output: Dog barks
    }
}
```

7. What is the role of the `super` keyword in Java? Explain with examples.

Answer:

The `super` keyword in Java refers to the immediate parent class of a subclass. It is used for the following purposes:

1. To call a constructor of the superclass.
2. To access superclass methods that have been overridden.
3. To access superclass fields.

Example:

```java
class Animal {
    String sound = "Animal makes sound";

    Animal() {
        System.out.println("Animal Constructor");
    }

    void display() {
        System.out.println("Animal Display");
    }
}

class Dog extends Animal {
    String sound = "Dog barks";

    Dog() {
        super();   // Calling superclass constructor
        System.out.println("Dog Constructor");
    }

    void display() {
        super.display();   // Calling superclass method
        System.out.println("Dog Display");
    }

    public static void main(String[] args) {
        Dog dog = new Dog();
        dog.display(); // Calls method from both Dog and Animal class
    }
}
```

8. Describe the concept of encapsulation in Java and explain how it provides data security.

Answer:

Encapsulation is the OOP concept of wrapping data (variables) and methods (functions) into a single unit known as a class. It restricts direct access to the class variables and allows modification of their values only through specific methods.

This concept provides **data security** by making fields private and providing public getter and setter methods to access and modify the values of those fields.

Example:

```
class Person {
    private String name;
    private int age;

    // Getter method for name
    public String getName() {
        return name;
    }

    // Setter method for name
    public void setName(String name) {
        this.name = name;
    }

    // Getter method for age
    public int getAge() {
        return age;
    }

    // Setter method for age
    public void setAge(int age) {
        if (age > 0) {
            this.age = age;
        } else {
            System.out.println("Invalid age");
        }
    }
}

public class Main {
    public static void main(String[] args) {
        Person person = new Person();
        person.setName("Alice");
        person.setAge(25);

        System.out.println("Name: " + person.getName());
        System.out.println("Age: " + person.getAge());
    }
}
```

In this example, the `Person` class uses encapsulation to protect the `name` and `age` fields by making them `private`, while allowing controlled access to these fields through getter and setter methods.

9. Explain the concept of constructor chaining in Java. How does it work?

Answer:

Constructor chaining in Java refers to the process of calling one constructor from another constructor within the same class or in the parent class. This can help avoid redundancy and ensure that all constructors follow a proper sequence.

Constructor chaining works with the `this()` and `super()` keywords:

- `this()` is used to call another constructor of the same class.
- `super()` is used to call a constructor of the parent class.

Example:

```java
class Person {
    String name;
    int age;

    // Constructor with two parameters
    Person(String name, int age) {
        this.name = name;
        this.age = age;
    }

    // Constructor with one parameter, calling the two-parameter constructor
    Person(String name) {
        this(name, 0);  // Calling the two-parameter constructor
    }

    void displayDetails() {
        System.out.println("Name: " + name);
        System.out.println("Age: " + age);
    }

    public static void main(String[] args) {
        Person person1 = new Person("Alice");
        person1.displayDetails();  // Age defaults to 0
    }
}
```

10. What is the `instanceof` operator in Java? Explain its usage with examples.

Answer:

The `instanceof` operator in Java is used to test whether an object is an instance of a specific class or subclass, or whether it implements a particular interface. It is commonly used to perform runtime type checking.

Example:

```
class Animal {}

class Dog extends Animal {}

public class Main {
    public static void main(String[] args) {
        Animal animal = new Dog();

        // Using instanceof to check type
        if (animal instanceof Dog) {
            System.out.println("This is a Dog object");
        }

        if (animal instanceof Animal) {
            System.out.println("This is an Animal object");
        }
    }
}
```

11. Explain the concept of method signature in Java. How does it relate to method overloading?

Answer:

A **method signature** in Java consists of:

1. **Method name**: The name of the method.
2. **Parameter list**: The number and types of parameters passed to the method.

The method signature does not include:

- Return type
- Access modifiers (like `public`, `private`)

Method overloading is possible because each overloaded method has a different method signature. This allows multiple methods to have the same name but different parameters.

Example:

```
class Calculator {
    int add(int a, int b) {
        return a + b;
    }

    double add(double a, double b) {
        return a + b;
    }
}
```

12. What is an interface in Java? How does it differ from an abstract class?

Answer:

An **interface** in Java is a reference type, similar to a class, that can contain only abstract methods (until Java 8) and constants. It is used to define a contract for what a class can do without specifying how it does it.

- **Interface**:
  - Cannot contain any implementation (except for default/static methods).
  - A class can implement multiple interfaces.
  - All methods in an interface are implicitly public and abstract.
- **Abstract class**:
  - Can contain both abstract (without implementation) and concrete (with implementation) methods.
  - A class can inherit only one abstract class.

Example:

```
interface Animal {
    void sound();   // Abstract method
}

class Dog implements Animal {
    @Override
    public void sound() {
        System.out.println("Barks");
    }
}
```

CHAPTER 4: ARRAYS AND STRINGS

30 multiple-choice questions (MCQs) ::

1. Which of the following is the correct syntax for declaring an array in Java?

a) `int[] arr = new int[5];`
b) `int arr = new int(5);`
c) `int arr[5];`
d) `int arr[] = int[5];`

Answer: a) `int[] arr = new int[5];`

---

2. What is the default value of an integer array element in Java?

a) 0
b) null
c) undefined
d) -1

Answer: a) 0

---

3. How can you find the length of an array in Java?

a) `array.size()`
b) `array.length()`
c) `array.length`
d) `array.getLength()`

Answer: c) `array.length`

---

4. Which of the following is the correct way to initialize a string array?

a) `String[] arr = new String[];`
b) `String[] arr = {"apple", "banana", "cherry"};`
c) `String arr[] = new String[3]{"apple", "banana", "cherry"};`
d) `String arr = {"apple", "banana", "cherry"};`

Answer: b) `String[] arr = {"apple", "banana", "cherry"};`

5. What is the index of the first element of an array in Java?

a) 1
b) 0
c) -1
d) None of the above

Answer: b) 0

6. Which method of the `Arrays` class can be used to sort an array in Java?

a) `Arrays.sort()`
b) `Arrays.order()`
c) `Arrays.sortArray()`
d) `Arrays.arrange()`

Answer: a) `Arrays.sort()`

7. What is the output of the following code?

```
String str = "Hello";
System.out.println(str.charAt(1));
```

a) `H`
b) `e`
c) `l`
d) `o`

Answer: b) `e`

8. Which of the following methods is used to compare two strings in Java?

a) `compareTo()`
b) `compare()`
c) `equals()`
d) Both a and c

Answer: d) Both a and c

---

9. What will be the output of the following code?

```
String str1 = "Java";
String str2 = "java";
System.out.println(str1.equals(str2));
```

a) `true`
b) `false`
c) `Java`
d) `java`

Answer: b) `false`

---

10. Which of the following is used to convert a string to uppercase in Java?

a) `toUpperCase()`
b) `toUpper()`
c) `convertToUpper()`
d) `upperCase()`

Answer: a) `toUpperCase()`

---

11. What will be the output of the following code?

```
String str = "Java Programming";
System.out.println(str.length());
```

a) `15`
b) `16`
c) `17`
d) `14`

Answer: b) `16`

---

12. How do you declare a 2D array in Java?

a) `int[][] arr;`
b) `int[] arr[];`
c) `int arr[][];`
d) All of the above

Answer: d) All of the above

---

13. Which of the following is the correct way to access the element at row 2, column 3 in a 2D array?

a) `array[2, 3]`
b) `array[2][3]`
c) `array[3][2]`
d) `array[3, 2]`

Answer: b) `array[2][3]`

---

14. Which method is used to find the index of a character in a string in Java?

a) `find()`
b) `getIndex()`
c) `indexOf()`
d) `search()`

Answer: c) `indexOf()`

---

15. Which of the following is the correct way to initialize an integer array of size 5 in Java?

a) `int arr = new int[5];`
b) `int arr[] = {1, 2, 3, 4, 5};`
c) `int[] arr = new int[5];`
d) Both b and c

Answer: d) Both b and c

---

16. Which of the following is a method in the `string` class that removes leading and trailing spaces?

a) `trim()`
b) `strip()`
c) `clear()`
d) `removeSpaces()`

Answer: a) `trim()`

---

17. What is the output of the following code?

```
String str = "Hello";
System.out.println(str.substring(1, 3));
```

a) `Hel`
b) `el`
c) `llo`
d) `Hello`

Answer: b) `el`

---

18. What will be the output of the following code?

```
int[] arr = {10, 20, 30};
System.out.println(arr[1]);
```

a) `10`
b) `20`
c) `30`
d) Compilation Error

Answer: b) `20`

---

19. Which of the following functions is used to convert a string to a character array in Java?

a) `toCharArray()`
b) `convertToCharArray()`

c) `getChars()`
d) `toCharacterArray()`

Answer: a) `toCharArray()`

---

20. What is the output of the following code?

```
String str = "Java Programming";
System.out.println(str.contains("Java"));
```

a) `true`
b) `false`
c) `Java`
d) `Programming`

Answer: a) `true`

---

21. Which of the following arrays is created correctly in Java?

a) `int[] arr = new int[3];`
b) `int arr[] = new int(3);`
c) `int[] arr = new int[3, 4];`
d) `int[] arr = new int[];`

Answer: a) `int[] arr = new int[3];`

---

22. Which of the following methods returns a part of the string from a specified index in Java?

a) `substring()`
b) `getPart()`
c) `split()`
d) `partition()`

Answer: a) `substring()`

---

23. Which of the following arrays is a valid declaration in Java?

```
a) int[] arr = new int[];
b) int[] arr = {};
c) int[] arr = new int[5] {1, 2, 3};
d) int[] arr = new int(5);
```

Answer: b) `int[] arr = {};`

---

24. What will be the result of the following expression in Java?

```
String str = "hello";
str = str.toUpperCase();
System.out.println(str);
```

a) `hello`
b) `HELLO`
c) `hEllo`
d) `Hello`

Answer: b) `HELLO`

---

25. Which of the following methods is used to split a string into an array in Java?

a) `split()`
b) `divide()`
c) `break()`
d) `substring()`

Answer: a) `split()`

---

26. What is the output of the following code?

```
String str = "abc";
System.out.println(str.equals("ABC"));
```

a) `true`
b) `false`
c) `abc`
d) `ABC`

Answer: b) `false`

---

27. What is the maximum number of elements that can be stored in an array in Java?

a) 1024
b) Integer.MAX_VALUE
c) 2147483647
d) 1000000

Answer: b) Integer.MAX_VALUE

---

28. Which of the following is true about the `String` class in Java?

a) String is immutable.
b) String is mutable.
c) String objects cannot be concatenated.
d) String objects are faster than StringBuilder.

Answer: a) String is immutable.

---

29. Which of the following will compile successfully?

a) `int arr[] = new int[5]; arr[0] = 10;`
b) `int[] arr = {1, 2, 3, 4, 5}; arr[6] = 10;`
c) `int arr[] = new int[5]; arr = {1, 2, 3};`
d) `int[] arr = new int[5]; arr[1.5] = 10;`

Answer: a) `int arr[] = new int[5]; arr[0] = 10;`

---

30. Which method of the `Arrays` class is used to fill an array with a specific value?

a) `Arrays.fill()`
b) `Arrays.initialize()`
c) `Arrays.set()`
d) `Arrays.update()`

Answer: a) `Arrays.fill()`

30 short questions with their answers:

1. What is an array in Java?

Answer: An array in Java is a collection of similar data types stored in a contiguous memory location.

2. How do you declare an array in Java?

Answer: You declare an array in Java using the syntax: `dataType[] arrayName;`

3. What is the default value of an element in an integer array in Java?

Answer: The default value of an integer array element is `0`.

4. What is the syntax for creating a string array?

Answer: A string array is created using: `String[] arr = new String[]{"a", "b", "c"};`

5. How do you find the length of an array in Java?

Answer: You use `array.length` to find the length of an array.

6. How can you access an element of an array in Java?

Answer: You access an element of an array using the syntax: `array[index]`.

7. What is the index of the first element in an array?

Answer: The index of the first element in an array is `0`.

8. What is the difference between `String` and `StringBuilder` in Java?

Answer: `String` is immutable, while `StringBuilder` is mutable and allows for modifying strings.

---

9. What method is used to compare two strings in Java?

Answer: You can use `equals()` or `compareTo()` to compare two strings.

---

10. How can you convert a string to an array of characters in Java?

Answer: Use the `toCharArray()` method to convert a string to a character array.

---

11. What is the purpose of the `split()` method in the `String` class?

Answer: The `split()` method splits a string into an array of substrings based on a specified delimiter.

---

12. How can you convert a string to uppercase in Java?

Answer: Use the `toUpperCase()` method to convert a string to uppercase.

---

13. What is the output of `str.charAt(2)` if `str = "Java"`?

Answer: The output is `v`, as it is the character at index 2.

---

14. How do you check if two strings are equal in Java?

Answer: Use `str1.equals(str2)` to check if two strings are equal.

---

15. What does the `indexOf()` method of the `String` class do?

Answer: The `indexOf()` method returns the index of the first occurrence of a specified character or substring in the string.

16. Can you change the size of an array after it is created?

Answer: No, the size of an array in Java is fixed once it is created.

17. What does the `substring()` method in the `string` class do?

Answer: The `substring()` method returns a new string that is a substring of the original string.

18. How do you declare a multidimensional array in Java?

Answer: A multidimensional array is declared using: `dataType[][] arrayName;`

19. What is the default value of an element in a boolean array in Java?

Answer: The default value of a boolean array element is `false`.

20. How do you initialize an array in Java?

Answer: You can initialize an array by specifying the values: `int[] arr = {1, 2, 3, 4};`

21. How do you get a substring of a string in Java?

Answer: Use `substring(startIndex, endIndex)` to get a substring of a string.

22. What will the following code output?

```
String str = "Hello";
System.out.println(str.length());
```

Answer: The output will be 5.

---

23. Can you store different data types in a single array in Java?

Answer: No, arrays in Java are of fixed type, meaning you can store only one data type in a single array.

---

24. What is the purpose of the `trim()` method in the `string` class?

Answer: The `trim()` method removes leading and trailing whitespace from a string.

---

25. What is the output of the following code?

```
String str = "apple";
System.out.println(str.substring(1, 3));
```

Answer: The output will be pp.

---

26. What is the difference between `StringBuilder` and `StringBuffer`?

Answer: Both are mutable, but `StringBuffer` is thread-safe, while `StringBuilder` is not.

---

27. What is the output of the following code?

```
String str = "Hello World!";
System.out.println(str.indexOf('o'));
```

Answer: The output will be 4, as 'o' is at index 4.

28. What method is used to convert a string to lowercase in Java?

Answer: Use the `toLowerCase()` method to convert a string to lowercase.

---

29. Can you assign a new size to an existing array in Java?

Answer: No, arrays in Java are fixed in size after creation, but you can create a new array of a different size.

---

30. What does the `Arrays.sort()` method do in Java?

Answer: The `Arrays.sort()` method sorts the elements of an array in ascending order.

15 practical questions with answers:

1. Write a program to find the largest element in an array.

Answer:

```java
public class LargestElement {
    public static void main(String[] args) {
        int[] arr = {5, 12, 78, 34, 23};
        int max = arr[0];

        for(int i = 1; i < arr.length; i++) {
            if(arr[i] > max) {
                max = arr[i];
            }
        }

        System.out.println("Largest element is: " + max);
    }
}
```

2. Write a program to reverse an array.

Answer:

```java
public class ReverseArray {
    public static void main(String[] args) {
        int[] arr = {1, 2, 3, 4, 5};
        int start = 0;
        int end = arr.length - 1;

        while (start < end) {
            int temp = arr[start];
            arr[start] = arr[end];
            arr[end] = temp;
            start++;
            end--;
        }

        System.out.println("Reversed array: ");
        for (int num : arr) {
            System.out.print(num + " ");
```

```
            }
        }
    }
```

3. Write a program to count the occurrences of a specific element in an array.

Answer:

```
public class CountOccurrences {
    public static void main(String[] args) {
        int[] arr = {1, 2, 2, 3, 2, 4};
        int count = 0;
        int element = 2;

        for(int i = 0; i < arr.length; i++) {
            if(arr[i] == element) {
                count++;
            }
        }

        System.out.println("Element " + element + " occurs " + count + "
times.");
    }
}
```

4. Write a program to merge two arrays.

Answer:

```
public class MergeArrays {
    public static void main(String[] args) {
        int[] arr1 = {1, 2, 3};
        int[] arr2 = {4, 5, 6};

        int[] mergedArr = new int[arr1.length + arr2.length];

        System.arraycopy(arr1, 0, mergedArr, 0, arr1.length);
        System.arraycopy(arr2, 0, mergedArr, arr1.length, arr2.length);

        System.out.println("Merged array: ");
        for (int num : mergedArr) {
            System.out.print(num + " ");
        }
    }
}
```

5. Write a program to check if a given string is a palindrome.

Answer:

```
public class Palindrome {
    public static void main(String[] args) {
        String str = "madam";
```

```
        String reversed = "";

        for (int i = str.length() - 1; i >= 0; i--) {
            reversed += str.charAt(i);
        }

        if(str.equals(reversed)) {
            System.out.println(str + " is a palindrome.");
        } else {
            System.out.println(str + " is not a palindrome.");
        }
    }
}
```

6. Write a program to find the second largest element in an array.

Answer:

```
public class SecondLargest {
    public static void main(String[] args) {
        int[] arr = {10, 20, 4, 45, 99};
        int first = Integer.MIN_VALUE;
        int second = Integer.MIN_VALUE;

        for (int num : arr) {
            if (num > first) {
                second = first;
                first = num;
            } else if (num > second && num != first) {
                second = num;
            }
        }

        System.out.println("Second largest element is: " + second);
    }
}
```

7. Write a program to remove all occurrences of a specific element from an array.

Answer:

```
import java.util.ArrayList;

public class RemoveElement {
    public static void main(String[] args) {
        int[] arr = {1, 2, 3, 4, 2, 5, 2};
        int element = 2;
        ArrayList<Integer> resultList = new ArrayList<>();

        for (int num : arr) {
            if (num != element) {
                resultList.add(num);
            }
```

```
        }
        System.out.println("Array after removing element " + element + ": " +
resultList);
    }
}
```

8. Write a program to check if two strings are anagrams of each other.

Answer:

```java
import java.util.Arrays;

public class AnagramCheck {
    public static void main(String[] args) {
        String str1 = "listen";
        String str2 = "silent";

        char[] str1Array = str1.toCharArray();
        char[] str2Array = str2.toCharArray();

        Arrays.sort(str1Array);
        Arrays.sort(str2Array);

        if (Arrays.equals(str1Array, str2Array)) {
            System.out.println(str1 + " and " + str2 + " are anagrams.");
        } else {
            System.out.println(str1 + " and " + str2 + " are not anagrams.");
        }
    }
}
```

9. Write a program to find the common elements between two arrays.

Answer:

```java
java
Copy
import java.util.HashSet;

public class CommonElements {
    public static void main(String[] args) {
        int[] arr1 = {1, 2, 3, 4, 5};
        int[] arr2 = {4, 5, 6, 7, 8};

        HashSet<Integer> set1 = new HashSet<>();
        for (int num : arr1) {
            set1.add(num);
        }

        System.out.println("Common elements:");
        for (int num : arr2) {
            if (set1.contains(num)) {
                System.out.println(num);
```

```
            }
        }
    }
}
```

10. Write a program to convert a string to an integer.

Answer:

```
public class StringToInt {
    public static void main(String[] args) {
        String str = "1234";
        int num = Integer.parseInt(str);
        System.out.println("Converted number: " + num);
    }
}
```

11. Write a program to concatenate two strings.

Answer:

```
public class ConcatenateStrings {
    public static void main(String[] args) {
        String str1 = "Hello";
        String str2 = " World!";

        String result = str1 + str2;
        System.out.println("Concatenated string: " + result);
    }
}
```

12. Write a program to find the frequency of each character in a string.

Answer:

```
import java.util.HashMap;

public class CharacterFrequency {
    public static void main(String[] args) {
        String str = "hello world";
        HashMap<Character, Integer> freqMap = new HashMap<>();

        for (char ch : str.toCharArray()) {
            freqMap.put(ch, freqMap.getOrDefault(ch, 0) + 1);
        }

        for (char key : freqMap.keySet()) {
            System.out.println(key + ": " + freqMap.get(key));
        }
    }
}
```

13. Write a program to sort an array in ascending order.

Answer:

```java
import java.util.Arrays;

public class SortArray {
    public static void main(String[] args) {
        int[] arr = {5, 2, 8, 1, 3};
        Arrays.sort(arr);

        System.out.println("Sorted array: ");
        for (int num : arr) {
            System.out.print(num + " ");
        }   } }
```

14. Write a program to find the first non-repeated character in a string.

Answer:

```java
import java.util.LinkedHashMap;

public class FirstNonRepeatedChar {
    public static void main(String[] args) {
        String str = "swiss";
        LinkedHashMap<Character, Integer> charCount = new LinkedHashMap<>();

        for (char ch : str.toCharArray()) {
            charCount.put(ch, charCount.getOrDefault(ch, 0) + 1);
        }

        for (char ch : charCount.keySet()) {
            if (charCount.get(ch) == 1) {
                System.out.println("First non-repeated character is: " + ch);
                break;
            }        }    }}
```

15. Write a program to check if a string contains only digits.

Answer:

```java
public class IsDigitsOnly {
    public static void main(String[] args) {
        String str = "12345";

        if (str.matches("[0-9]+")) {
            System.out.println(str + " contains only digits.");
        } else {
            System.out.println(str + " contains non-digit characters.");
        }
    }
}
```

12 long-answer questions with answers :

1. Explain the concept of arrays in Java. How do you declare and initialize an array? Provide examples.

Answer:

An **array** in Java is a data structure that allows storing multiple values of the same type. It is a container object that holds a fixed number of values of a single type. Arrays are indexed, meaning each element in an array is accessed by a numeric index, starting from 0.

Declaring and Initializing Arrays:

- **Declaration:** To declare an array, you specify the type of elements the array will hold, followed by square brackets [], and the variable name.

  Example:

  ```
  int[] arr; // Declaring an integer array
  ```

- **Initialization:** Arrays can be initialized at the time of declaration or later.

  Example:

  ```
  int[] arr = new int[5]; // Declaring an array with 5 elements, default
  value 0
  ```

  You can also initialize an array with values at the time of declaration:

  ```
  int[] arr = {10, 20, 30, 40, 50}; // Initializing an array with values
  ```

Arrays in Java are **fixed in size**, meaning once they are initialized, the size cannot be changed.

2. What are multi-dimensional arrays in Java? How do you declare and access them?

Answer:

A **multi-dimensional array** is an array of arrays. In Java, you can create arrays with more than one dimension, typically 2D (matrix) or 3D.

Declaring and Initializing Multi-Dimensional Arrays:

- A 2D array can be declared as:

  ```
  int[][] matrix; // Declaration of a 2D array
  ```

- To create and initialize a 2D array:

```
int[][] matrix = new int[3][3]; // 3x3 matrix
```

- You can also initialize it with values at the time of declaration:

```
int[][] matrix = {
    {1, 2, 3},
    {4, 5, 6},
    {7, 8, 9}
};
```

Accessing Elements:

To access elements in a multi-dimensional array, you use two (or more) indices. For example:

```
System.out.println(matrix[1][2]); // Accesses the element in the second row,
third column (value 6 in this case)
```

3. How do you find the length of an array in Java? Explain with an example.

Answer:

In Java, you can find the length of an array using the `length` property of the array. This property returns the number of elements present in the array.

Example:

```
int[] arr = {10, 20, 30, 40, 50};
System.out.println("Length of the array is: " + arr.length);
```

The output will be:

```
Length of the array is: 5
```

Note that `arr.length` gives the number of elements, not the highest index of the array.

4. What are the differences between Arrays and ArrayLists in Java?

Answer:

Arrays and **ArrayLists** are both used to store elements in Java, but there are several key differences between them:

- **Size:**
    - Arrays have a fixed size. Once you declare the size of an array, it cannot be changed.

- ○ ArrayLists are dynamic, meaning their size can grow or shrink during runtime.
- **Type:**
  - ○ Arrays can store elements of any type (primitive or objects).
  - ○ ArrayLists can only store objects, so primitive types need to be wrapped in corresponding wrapper classes (e.g., `int` becomes `Integer`).
- **Performance:**
  - ○ Arrays are faster in terms of performance for simple operations due to their fixed size.
  - ○ ArrayLists may have a slight overhead due to dynamic resizing.
- **Flexibility:**
  - ○ Arrays are suitable when you know the exact number of elements beforehand.
  - ○ ArrayLists are ideal when you need to frequently add or remove elements.

Example:

```
// Array example
int[] arr = {1, 2, 3};

// ArrayList example
import java.util.ArrayList;
ArrayList<Integer> list = new ArrayList<>();
list.add(1);
list.add(2);
list.add(3);
```

5. Explain how to sort an array in Java. Provide an example using the `Arrays.sort()` method.

Answer:

The `Arrays.sort()` method in Java is used to sort an array in ascending order. This method belongs to the `java.util.Arrays` class.

Example:

```
import java.util.Arrays;

public class SortArray {
    public static void main(String[] args) {
        int[] arr = {4, 2, 8, 5, 1};

        // Sorting the array
        Arrays.sort(arr);

        // Printing the sorted array
        System.out.println("Sorted array: " + Arrays.toString(arr));
    }
}
```

Output:

```
Sorted array: [1, 2, 4, 5, 8]
```

By default, `Arrays.sort()` sorts arrays in ascending order. For descending order, you can use a custom comparator or reverse the array after sorting.

6. How do you compare two strings in Java? What is the difference between == and `.equals()` method?

Answer:

In Java, two strings can be compared using either the == operator or the `.equals()` method, but these two behave differently:

- ==: This operator compares the **reference** of the two strings, meaning it checks whether both references point to the same memory location.

  Example:

  ```
  String str1 = new String("hello");
  String str2 = new String("hello");
  System.out.println(str1 == str2); // false, because they are different
  objects
  ```

- `.equals()`: This method compares the **content** of the two strings, meaning it checks whether the two strings have the same characters in the same order.

  Example:

  ```
  String str1 = "hello";
  String str2 = "hello";
  System.out.println(str1.equals(str2)); // true, because the contents
  are the same
  ```

7. How do you concatenate two strings in Java? Provide examples of different ways to do it.

Answer:

In Java, you can concatenate strings using several methods:

- **Using the + operator:**

  ```
  String str1 = "Hello ";
  String str2 = "World!";
  String result = str1 + str2;
  System.out.println(result); // Output: "Hello World!"
  ```

- **Using the `concat()` method:**

```
String str1 = "Hello ";
String str2 = "World!";
String result = str1.concat(str2);
System.out.println(result); // Output: "Hello World!"
```

- **Using `StringBuilder` or `StringBuffer`:** String concatenation using `StringBuilder` or `StringBuffer` is more efficient, especially in loops, because it doesn't create multiple intermediate string objects.

```
StringBuilder sb = new StringBuilder();
sb.append("Hello ");
sb.append("World!");
System.out.println(sb.toString()); // Output: "Hello World!"
```

8. How can you convert a string to an integer in Java?

Answer:

To convert a string to an integer in Java, you can use the `Integer.parseInt()` method. This method takes a string as an argument and returns its integer equivalent.

Example:

```
String str = "123";
int num = Integer.parseInt(str);
System.out.println("Converted number: " + num); // Output: "Converted number:
123"
```

If the string cannot be converted to an integer (i.e., it contains non-numeric characters), this method will throw a `NumberFormatException`. You can handle this using a `try-catch` block.

9. Explain the concept of string immutability in Java.

Answer:

In Java, **strings are immutable**, meaning once a string object is created, it cannot be modified. Any operation that appears to modify a string actually creates a new string object. This property is crucial for several reasons, including thread safety and performance optimization in memory management.

Example:

```
String str = "hello";
str = str.concat(" world"); // This creates a new string object
System.out.println(str); // Output: "hello world"
```

In the above example, the original string `"hello"` remains unchanged. The `concat()` method creates a new string, and `str` now references the new string `"hello world"`.

10. How do you find the length of a string in Java?

Answer:

In Java, you can find the length of a string using the `length()` method. This method returns the number of characters present in the string.

Example:

```
String str = "Java Programming";
int length = str.length();
System.out.println("Length of the string: " + length); // Output: "Length of
the string: 17"
```

The `length()` method counts all characters, including spaces, punctuation, and special characters.

11. What is a substring? How do you extract a substring from a string in Java?

Answer:

A **substring** is a portion of a string. In Java, you can extract a substring using the `substring()` method, which is part of the `String` class.

Example:

```
String str = "Java Programming";
String subStr = str.substring(5, 16); // Extracting substring from index 5 to
15
System.out.println("Substring: " + subStr); // Output: "Programming"
```

The `substring()` method takes two parameters: the starting index (inclusive) and the ending index (exclusive).

12. How do you search for a character or substring in a string in Java?

Answer:

In Java, you can use the `indexOf()` or `contains()` methods to search for a character or substring within a string.

- **Using `indexOf()`:** It returns the index of the first occurrence of the character or substring.

  Example:

  ```
  String str = "Java Programming";
  ```

```
int index = str.indexOf("Pro");
System.out.println("Index of 'Pro': " + index); // Output: "Index of
'Pro': 5"
```

- **Using `contains()`:** It returns `true` if the substring is found, otherwise `false`.

  Example:

  ```
  String str = "Java Programming";
  boolean contains = str.contains("Java");
  System.out.println("Contains 'Java': " + contains); // Output:
  "Contains 'Java': true"
  ```

CHAPTER 5: EXCEPTION HANDLING

30 MCQs:

---

1. What is an exception in Java?

a) An event that disrupts the normal flow of a program
b) A type of method
c) An object of a class
d) A condition that can always be ignored

Answer: a) An event that disrupts the normal flow of a program

---

2. Which of the following is the superclass of all errors and exceptions in Java?

a) Throwable
b) Error
c) Exception
d) Object

Answer: a) Throwable

---

3. Which of the following keywords is used to handle exceptions in Java?

a) catch
b) throw
c) try
d) All of the above

Answer: d) All of the above

---

4. What is the purpose of the `try` block in Java exception handling?

a) To throw an exception
b) To catch an exception
c) To define a block of code where exceptions may occur
d) To handle a specific type of exception

Answer: c) To define a block of code where exceptions may occur

---

5. Which keyword is used to explicitly throw an exception in Java?

a) throws
b) catch
c) throw
d) try

Answer: c) throw

---

6. Which of the following exceptions are checked exceptions?

a) ArithmeticException
b) NullPointerException
c) IOException
d) ArrayIndexOutOfBoundsException

Answer: c) IOException

---

7. Which of the following statements about `finally` block is true?

a) The `finally` block is executed only when an exception occurs.
b) The `finally` block is executed only when no exception occurs.
c) The `finally` block is always executed, regardless of an exception.
d) The `finally` block is not executed if an exception is thrown.

Answer: c) The `finally` block is always executed, regardless of an exception.

---

8. What is the output of the following code?

```
try {
    System.out.println(10 / 0);
} catch (ArithmeticException e) {
    System.out.println("ArithmeticException");
} finally {
    System.out.println("Finally block");
}
```

a) ArithmeticException
b) 0
c) Finally block
d) ArithmeticException Finally block

Answer: d) ArithmeticException Finally block

---

9. Which exception is thrown when a program tries to divide a number by zero?

a) ArithmeticException
b) NullPointerException
c) ArrayIndexOutOfBoundsException
d) NumberFormatException

Answer: a) ArithmeticException

---

10. Which of the following is a runtime exception?

a) IOException
b) SQLException
c) NullPointerException
d) ClassNotFoundException

Answer: c) NullPointerException

---

11. Which of the following keywords is used to define a method that may throw an exception?

a) throws
b) throw
c) try
d) catch

Answer: a) throws

---

12. What happens when an exception is not caught in Java?

a) The program continues running
b) The program terminates
c) The exception is automatically resolved
d) A warning is displayed

Answer: b) The program terminates

---

13. Which exception is thrown when an array is accessed with an invalid index?

a) ArrayIndexOutOfBoundsException
b) NullPointerException
c) IllegalArgumentException
d) ArithmeticException

Answer: a) ArrayIndexOutOfBoundsException

---

14. Which of the following will cause a `NullPointerException`?

a) Accessing a null object reference
b) Dividing a number by zero
c) Accessing an invalid index of an array
d) Using an invalid class type

Answer: a) Accessing a null object reference

---

15. Which method of `Exception` class returns the message of the exception?

a) getMessage()
b) getStackTrace()
c) printStackTrace()
d) toString()

Answer: a) getMessage()

---

16. What is the base class for all exceptions in Java?

a) Throwable
b) Error

c) Exception
d) Object

Answer: c) Exception

---

17. What will happen if you don't catch an exception in Java?

a) The program will stop executing
b) The JVM will catch the exception automatically
c) The program will execute without any issues
d) An error message will be displayed

Answer: a) The program will stop executing

---

18. Which type of exceptions can be handled using the `throws` keyword?

a) Runtime exceptions
b) Checked exceptions
c) Both checked and unchecked exceptions
d) Only `Error` exceptions

Answer: b) Checked exceptions

---

19. Which of the following is not a type of exception in Java?

a) RuntimeException
b) Error
c) Exception
d) ExceptionHandler

Answer: d) ExceptionHandler

---

20. Which of the following statements is correct about `throw` and `throws` in Java?

a) `throw` is used to declare an exception, and `throws` is used to throw an exception.
b) `throw` is used to throw an exception, and `throws` is used to declare an exception.

c) Both `throw` and `throws` are used interchangeably.
d) Neither `throw` nor `throws` can be used in Java.

Answer: b) `throw` is used to throw an exception, and `throws` is used to declare an exception.

---

21. Which of the following is the correct way to handle multiple exceptions in a single `catch` block (introduced in Java 7)?

a) catch (Exception1 | Exception2 e) { }
b) catch (Exception1 & Exception2 e) { }
c) catch (Exception1, Exception2 e) { }
d) catch (Exception1 and Exception2 e) { }

Answer: a) catch (Exception1 | Exception2 e) { }

---

22. Which of the following exceptions is thrown when a program tries to access an object reference that has not been initialized?

a) NullPointerException
b) ArithmeticException
c) IndexOutOfBoundsException
d) ClassNotFoundException

Answer: a) NullPointerException

---

23. What is the purpose of the `finally` block in Java?

a) It is used to throw exceptions
b) It is used to catch exceptions
c) It is used to execute code regardless of whether an exception occurs or not
d) It is used to declare exceptions

Answer: c) It is used to execute code regardless of whether an exception occurs or not

---

24. Which of the following is an unchecked exception?

a) IOException
b) ClassNotFoundException
c) NullPointerException
d) FileNotFoundException

Answer: c) NullPointerException

---

25. Which of the following classes is used to handle input/output exceptions?

a) IOException
b) SQLException
c) FileNotFoundException
d) ArithmeticException

Answer: a) IOException

---

26. How can you handle multiple exceptions in a single `catch` block in Java?

a) By using multiple `catch` blocks
b) By using the `|` (OR) operator
c) By using the `&` (AND) operator
d) By declaring exceptions inside a `finally` block

Answer: b) By using the `|` (OR) operator

---

27. Which of the following statements about the `throw` keyword is true?

a) The `throw` keyword is used to declare an exception
b) The `throw` keyword is used to create a new exception
c) The `throw` keyword is used to handle exceptions
d) The `throw` keyword is used for automatic exception handling

Answer: b) The `throw` keyword is used to create a new exception

---

28. Which of the following is true regarding checked exceptions?

a) They are subclass of `RuntimeException`
b) They are subclass of `Error`
c) They must be either caught or declared using the `throws` keyword
d) They are not required to be handled in any way

Answer: c) They must be either caught or declared using the `throws` keyword

29. What is the result of executing the following code?

```
try {
    System.out.println("try block");
} finally {
    System.out.println("finally block");
}
```

a) try block will be printed only
b) finally block will be printed only
c) Both try and finally blocks will be printed
d) An exception will occur

Answer: c) Both try and finally blocks will be printed

30. Which of the following statements about exceptions in Java is correct?

a) Every exception class is a subclass of `RuntimeException`
b) Exceptions must always be declared using the `throws` keyword
c) Java uses exception handling to make programs more robust by recovering from errors
d) Exceptions do not terminate the program if they are handled correctly

Answer: c) Java uses exception handling to make programs more robust by recovering from errors

30 short questions and their answers:

1. What is an exception in Java?

Answer: An exception is an event that disrupts the normal flow of a program's execution.

2. What is the difference between checked and unchecked exceptions?

Answer: Checked exceptions are exceptions that are checked at compile-time, while unchecked exceptions are those that occur at runtime.

---

3. Which class is the superclass of all exceptions in Java?

Answer: The `Throwable` class is the superclass of all exceptions.

---

4. What is the use of the `try` block in Java?

Answer: The `try` block is used to define a block of code where exceptions may occur.

---

5. What is the purpose of the `catch` block?

Answer: The `catch` block is used to handle exceptions thrown by the `try` block.

---

6. What is the `finally` block used for?

Answer: The `finally` block is used to execute code that must run regardless of whether an exception occurred or not.

---

7. What will happen if no `catch` block is provided?

Answer: If no `catch` block is provided, the exception is propagated to the calling method. If not handled, the program terminates.

---

8. What is the difference between `throw` and `throws`?

Answer: `throw` is used to explicitly throw an exception, while `throws` is used to declare that a method may throw exceptions.

---

9. What is an example of a checked exception?

Answer: An example of a checked exception is `IOException`.

---

10. What is an example of an unchecked exception?

Answer: An example of an unchecked exception is `NullPointerException`.

---

11. What is the `getMessage()` method used for?

Answer: The `getMessage()` method is used to retrieve the message associated with an exception.

---

12. What is a runtime exception?

Answer: A runtime exception is an exception that occurs during the execution of the program, typically due to programming errors, such as `NullPointerException`.

---

13. What is the purpose of the `throws` keyword in Java?

Answer: The `throws` keyword is used to declare exceptions that a method may throw during its execution.

---

14. What will happen if a `finally` block has a return statement?

Answer: A `return` statement in the `finally` block will override any return statement from the `try` or `catch` block.

---

15. Can we handle multiple exceptions in one `catch` block in Java?

Answer: Yes, in Java 7 and above, we can handle multiple exceptions in a single `catch` block using the | operator.

16. What is an error in Java?

Answer: An error is a subclass of `Throwable` and represents serious issues that a program cannot handle, such as `OutOfMemoryError`.

17. How do you handle multiple exceptions with separate handling in Java?

Answer: You can handle multiple exceptions separately by using multiple `catch` blocks, each for a different exception type.

18. What happens if an exception is not caught in Java?

Answer: If an exception is not caught, it is propagated up the call stack. If uncaught, the program terminates.

19. What will happen if the `catch` block does not specify the exception type?

Answer: The program will give a compile-time error because a `catch` block must specify an exception type to handle.

20. Can we throw an exception from a `finally` block?

Answer: Yes, an exception can be thrown from a `finally` block, but it will override any exception thrown in the `try` block.

21. What is the `printStackTrace()` method used for?

Answer: The `printStackTrace()` method prints the stack trace of the exception, showing the sequence of method calls leading to the exception.

22. What is the superclass of `IOException`?

Answer: The superclass of `IOException` is `Exception`.

---

23. Is `NullPointerException` a checked or unchecked exception?

Answer: `NullPointerException` is an unchecked exception.

---

24. Can you catch `Error` in Java?

Answer: It is possible to catch `Error` objects, but it is generally not recommended since they indicate serious problems that are beyond the scope of normal exception handling.

---

25. What is the output of the following code?

```
try {
    System.out.println(5 / 0);
} catch (ArithmeticException e) {
    System.out.println("Exception caught");
} finally {
    System.out.println("Finally block");
}
```

Answer: The output will be:

```
Exception caught
Finally block
```

---

26. What does `throw` do in Java?

Answer: `throw` is used to explicitly throw an exception from a method or block of code.

---

27. What happens if the `finally` block throws an exception?

Answer: If the `finally` block throws an exception, it will override any exception thrown in the `try` block or `catch` block.

---

28. What is the exception thrown if a method calls another method with a `null` object reference?

Answer: A `NullPointerException` is thrown.

29. Can `catch` blocks handle multiple exceptions in a single block?

Answer: Yes, from Java 7 onward, multiple exceptions can be handled in a single `catch` block using the pipe | operator.

30. What is the difference between `Exception` and `Throwable`?

Answer: `Throwable` is the superclass of all errors and exceptions in Java, while `Exception` is a subclass of `Throwable` that represents exceptional conditions that a program should catch.

12 practical questions and their answers:

1. Write a Java program that catches an `ArithmeticException` when dividing by zero.

Answer:

```
public class ArithmeticExceptionExample {
    public static void main(String[] args) {
        try {
            int result = 10 / 0;
        } catch (ArithmeticException e) {
            System.out.println("Exception caught: " + e);        }    }}
```

Output:

```
Exception caught: java.lang.ArithmeticException: / by zero
```

2. Write a Java program that handles multiple exceptions using multiple `catch` blocks.

Answer:

```
public class MultipleCatchExample {
```

```java
    public static void main(String[] args) {
        try {
            int[] arr = new int[5];
            arr[10] = 30;   // ArrayIndexOutOfBoundsException
            int result = 10 / 0;   // ArithmeticException
        } catch (ArrayIndexOutOfBoundsException e) {
            System.out.println("Array Index Out of Bounds: " + e);
        } catch (ArithmeticException e) {
            System.out.println("Arithmetic Exception: " + e);
        }
    }
}
```

Output:

```
Array Index Out of Bounds: java.lang.ArrayIndexOutOfBoundsException: Index 10
out of bounds for length 5
```

3. Write a Java program that demonstrates the use of the `finally` block.

Answer:

```java
public class FinallyExample {
    public static void main(String[] args) {
        try {
            System.out.println("Inside try block");
        } catch (Exception e) {
            System.out.println("Inside catch block");
        } finally {
            System.out.println("Inside finally block");
        }
    }
}
```

Output:

```
Inside try block
Inside finally block
```

4. Write a program that throws an `ArrayIndexOutOfBoundsException` manually using the `throw` keyword.

Answer:

```java
public class ThrowExample {
    public static void main(String[] args) {
        try {
            throw new ArrayIndexOutOfBoundsException("Thrown manually");
        } catch (ArrayIndexOutOfBoundsException e) {
            System.out.println("Exception caught: " + e);
```

```
            }
        }
    }
```

Output:

```
Exception caught: java.lang.ArrayIndexOutOfBoundsException: Thrown manually
```

5. Write a Java program that catches and prints the stack trace of a NullPointerException.

Answer:

```java
public class NullPointerExceptionExample {
    public static void main(String[] args) {
        try {
            String str = null;
            System.out.println(str.length());
        } catch (NullPointerException e) {
            e.printStackTrace();
        }
    }
}
```

Output:

```
java.lang.NullPointerException
    at NullPointerExceptionExample.main(NullPointerExceptionExample.java:4)
```

6. Write a Java program to demonstrate exception propagation.

Answer:

```java
public class ExceptionPropagationExample {
    public static void main(String[] args) {
        try {
            method1();
        } catch (Exception e) {
            System.out.println("Exception caught in main: " + e);
        }
    }

    static void method1() throws Exception {
        method2();
    }

    static void method2() throws Exception {
        throw new Exception("Exception thrown in method2");
    }
}
```

Output:

```
Exception caught in main: java.lang.Exception: Exception thrown in method2
```

7. Write a Java program that uses `throws` keyword to declare an exception in the method signature.

Answer:

```java
public class ThrowsKeywordExample {
    public static void main(String[] args) {
        try {
            methodThatThrows();
        } catch (Exception e) {
            System.out.println("Exception caught: " + e);
        }
    }

    static void methodThatThrows() throws Exception {
        throw new Exception("Exception thrown from method");
    }
}
```

Output:

```
Exception caught: java.lang.Exception: Exception thrown from method
```

8. Write a program that demonstrates how to handle multiple exceptions in a single `catch` block.

Answer:

```java
public class MultiCatchExample {
    public static void main(String[] args) {
        try {
            String str = null;
            System.out.println(str.length());
            int result = 10 / 0;
        } catch (NullPointerException | ArithmeticException e) {
            System.out.println("Exception caught: " + e);
        }
    }
}
```

Output:

```
Exception caught: java.lang.NullPointerException
```

9. Write a Java program to demonstrate the use of `getMessage()` method with exception objects.

Answer:

```
public class GetMessageExample {
    public static void main(String[] args) {
        try {
            int[] arr = new int[5];
            arr[10] = 20; // ArrayIndexOutOfBoundsException
        } catch (ArrayIndexOutOfBoundsException e) {
            System.out.println("Exception message: " + e.getMessage());
        }
    }
}
```

Output:

```
pgsql
Copy
Exception message: Index 10 out of bounds for length 5
```

10. Write a program to catch and handle a `FileNotFoundException`.

Answer:

```
import java.io.*;

public class FileNotFoundExceptionExample {
    public static void main(String[] args) {
        try {
            FileReader file = new FileReader("nonexistentfile.txt");
        } catch (FileNotFoundException e) {
            System.out.println("File not found: " + e);
        }
    }
}
```

Output:

```
File not found: java.io.FileNotFoundException: nonexistentfile.txt (The
system cannot find the file specified)
```

11. Write a Java program that handles `IOException` using the `try-catch` block.

Answer:

```
import java.io.*;
```

```
public class IOExceptionExample {
    public static void main(String[] args) {
        try {
            FileReader file = new FileReader("testfile.txt");
            BufferedReader br = new BufferedReader(file);
            br.readLine();
            br.close();
        } catch (IOException e) {
            System.out.println("IOException occurred: " + e);
        }
    }
}
```

Output:

```
IOException occurred: java.io.FileNotFoundException: testfile.txt (The system
cannot find the file specified)
```

12. Write a program that demonstrates the use of a `custom exception` in Java.

Answer:

```
class AgeException extends Exception {
    public AgeException(String message) {
        super(message);
    }
}

public class CustomExceptionExample {
    public static void main(String[] args) {
        try {
            validateAge(15);
        } catch (AgeException e) {
            System.out.println("Exception caught: " + e.getMessage());
        }
    }

    static void validateAge(int age) throws AgeException {
        if (age < 18) {
            throw new AgeException("Age must be 18 or older.");
        }
    }
}
```

Output:

```
Exception caught: Age must be 18 or older.
```

10 long-length questions with detailed answers:

1. What is exception handling in Java? Explain the use of try, catch, throw, throws, and finally with examples.

Answer: Exception handling in Java is a powerful mechanism that allows us to handle runtime errors, ensuring the normal flow of the application. It helps in catching exceptions, debugging, and keeping the application stable.

- **try block**: A block of code that might throw an exception.
- **catch block**: Used to handle the exception that is thrown in the try block.
- **throw keyword**: Used to explicitly throw an exception from a method or block of code.
- **throws keyword**: Used to declare that a method can throw exceptions, thus passing the responsibility of handling them to the calling method.
- **finally block**: Contains code that will always execute, whether an exception is thrown or not, commonly used for cleanup actions like closing files, streams, etc.

Example:

```java
import java.io.*;

public class ExceptionHandlingExample {
    public static void main(String[] args) {
        try {
            FileReader file = new FileReader("test.txt");
            BufferedReader br = new BufferedReader(file);
            String line = br.readLine();
            br.close();
        } catch (FileNotFoundException e) {
            System.out.println("File not found: " + e.getMessage());
        } catch (IOException e) {
            System.out.println("IOException occurred: " + e.getMessage());
        } finally {
            System.out.println("This will always execute.");
        }
    }
}
```

In this example, if the file does not exist, `FileNotFoundException` is caught, and if there's an error in reading the file, `IOException` is caught. The `finally` block executes regardless of whether an exception occurs or not.

---

2. What is the difference between `throw` and `throws` in Java? Provide examples to illustrate both.

Answer:

- **throw**: The `throw` keyword is used to explicitly throw an exception. It is followed by an instance of the exception class.

- **throws**: The `throws` keyword is used in a method signature to declare that the method might throw one or more exceptions, passing the responsibility of handling them to the calling method.

Example using `throw`:

```java
public class ThrowExample {
    public static void checkAge(int age) {
        if (age < 18) {
            throw new ArithmeticException("Age must be 18 or older.");
        }
    }

    public static void main(String[] args) {
        try {
            checkAge(15);
        } catch (ArithmeticException e) {
            System.out.println(e.getMessage());
        }
    }
}
```

Example using `throws`:

```java
import java.io.*;

public class ThrowsExample {
    public static void readFile() throws IOException {
        FileReader file = new FileReader("nonexistent.txt");
    }

    public static void main(String[] args) {
        try {
            readFile();
        } catch (IOException e) {
            System.out.println("IOException caught: " + e);
        }
    }
}
```

In the first example, `throw` is used to throw an exception manually, and in the second example, `throws` is used to declare that the method `readFile` may throw an `IOException`.

---

3. Explain the concept of exception propagation in Java with an example.

Answer: Exception propagation in Java refers to the mechanism where an exception that occurs in a method is passed to the calling method until it is caught or handled. If a method doesn't handle an exception, it is passed to the calling method until it is eventually handled or propagated to the JVM.

Example:

```
public class ExceptionPropagationExample {
    public static void main(String[] args) {
        try {
            method1();
        } catch (Exception e) {
            System.out.println("Exception handled in main method: " + e);
        }
    }

    static void method1() throws Exception {
        method2();
    }

    static void method2() throws Exception {
        throw new Exception("Exception thrown from method2");
    }
}
```

In this example, `method1` calls `method2`, and if `method2` throws an exception, it propagates to `method1`, which then passes it to the `main` method for handling.

---

4. What is the significance of the `finally` block in exception handling? Can a `finally` block be skipped?

Answer: The `finally` block is used to execute essential code after a try-catch block, such as resource cleanup. It is guaranteed to execute, regardless of whether an exception was thrown or not. This block is particularly useful for closing resources like files, sockets, or database connections.

Can a `finally` block be skipped? The `finally` block will always execute unless:

- The JVM crashes.
- The `System.exit()` method is called.
- The thread executing the `finally` block is interrupted.

Example:

```
public class FinallyExample {
    public static void main(String[] args) {
        try {
            System.out.println("Inside try block");
        } catch (Exception e) {
            System.out.println("Inside catch block");
        } finally {
            System.out.println("Inside finally block");
        }
    }
}
```

```
}
```

Output:

```
Inside try block
Inside finally block
```

Even if no exception is thrown, the `finally` block will still execute.

---

5. What are custom exceptions in Java? How do you create and use a custom exception?

Answer: Custom exceptions are user-defined exceptions that extend the `Exception` class or any of its subclasses. They allow developers to throw and handle exceptions that are specific to the application's domain.

Steps to create a custom exception:

1. Define a new class that extends the `Exception` class.
2. Provide constructors to initialize the exception message or cause.

Example:

```java
class AgeException extends Exception {
    public AgeException(String message) {
        super(message);
    }
}

public class CustomExceptionExample {
    public static void validateAge(int age) throws AgeException {
        if (age < 18) {
            throw new AgeException("Age must be 18 or older.");
        }
    }

    public static void main(String[] args) {
        try {
            validateAge(15);
        } catch (AgeException e) {
            System.out.println("Exception caught: " + e.getMessage());
        }
    }
}
```

Output:

```
Exception caught: Age must be 18 or older.
```

In this example, the `AgeException` is a custom exception, and it is thrown and handled in the `main` method.

6. Explain the difference between `checked exceptions` and `unchecked exceptions`. Provide examples.

Answer:

- **Checked exceptions**: These exceptions are checked at compile-time. The programmer is required to handle or declare them using `throws`. Example: `IOException`, `SQLException`.
- **Unchecked exceptions**: These exceptions are not checked at compile-time. They are typically caused by programming errors. Example: `NullPointerException`, `ArrayIndexOutOfBoundsException`.

Example of checked exception:

```java
import java.io.*;

public class CheckedExceptionExample {
    public static void readFile() throws IOException {
        FileReader file = new FileReader("nonexistentfile.txt");
    }

    public static void main(String[] args) {
        try {
            readFile();
        } catch (IOException e) {
            System.out.println("IOException caught: " + e);
        }
    }
}
```

Example of unchecked exception:

```java
public class UncheckedExceptionExample {
    public static void main(String[] args) {
        String str = null;
        System.out.println(str.length());  // NullPointerException
    }
}
```

7. What is the purpose of the `getMessage()` and `printStackTrace()` methods in the Exception class?

Answer:

- **getMessage()**: Returns a detailed message string about the exception.
- **printStackTrace()**: Prints the stack trace of the exception to the standard error stream, which helps in debugging by showing where the exception occurred.

Example:

```java
public class ExceptionMethodsExample {
    public static void main(String[] args) {
        try {
            int[] arr = new int[2];
            arr[5] = 10;   // ArrayIndexOutOfBoundsException
        } catch (ArrayIndexOutOfBoundsException e) {
            System.out.println("Error message: " + e.getMessage());
            e.printStackTrace();
        }
    }
}
```

Output:

```
Error message: Index 5 out of bounds for length 2
java.lang.ArrayIndexOutOfBoundsException: Index 5 out of bounds for length 2
    at ExceptionMethodsExample.main(ExceptionMethodsExample.java:5)
```

8. How can you rethrow an exception in Java? What is the purpose of rethrowing an exception?

Answer: Rethrowing an exception means throwing an exception again after catching it. This can be useful when you want to log the exception, perform cleanup operations, and then allow the exception to propagate further.

Example:

```java
public class RethrowExample {
    public static void process() throws Exception {
        try {
            throw new Exception("Initial exception");
        } catch (Exception e) {
            System.out.println("Caught exception: " + e.getMessage());
            throw e;   // Rethrow the exception
        }
    }

    public static void main(String[] args) {
        try {
            process();
        } catch (Exception e) {
            System.out.println("Exception handled in main: " +
e.getMessage());
        }
    }
```

```
}
```

Output:

```
Caught exception: Initial exception
Exception handled in main: Initial exception
```

---

9. What are `nested try-catch` blocks? How are they used in exception handling?

Answer: A `nested try-catch` block is a try-catch block inside another try block. This is useful when different blocks of code might throw different types of exceptions, and you want to handle them separately.

Example:

```java
public class NestedTryCatchExample {
    public static void main(String[] args) {
        try {
            try {
                int result = 10 / 0;   // ArithmeticException
            } catch (ArithmeticException e) {
                System.out.println("Caught ArithmeticException");
            }

            int[] arr = new int[3];
            arr[5] = 30;   // ArrayIndexOutOfBoundsException
        } catch (ArrayIndexOutOfBoundsException e) {
            System.out.println("Caught ArrayIndexOutOfBoundsException");
        }
    }
}
```

Output:

```
Caught ArithmeticException
Caught ArrayIndexOutOfBoundsException
```

---

10. Explain how to handle multiple exceptions in a single catch block using Java 7's multi-catch feature.

Answer: Starting from Java 7, you can handle multiple exceptions in a single catch block by using the | (pipe) symbol. This feature helps to simplify the code when multiple exceptions are handled in the same way.

Example:

```java
public class MultiCatchExample {
    public static void main(String[] args) {
```

```
        try {
            String str = null;
            System.out.println(str.length());   // NullPointerException
            int result = 10 / 0;   // ArithmeticException
        } catch (NullPointerException | ArithmeticException e) {
            System.out.println("Exception caught: " + e);
        }
    }
}
```

Output:

```
Exception caught: java.lang.NullPointerException
```

This allows both `NullPointerException` and `ArithmeticException` to be handled by the same catch block.

CHAPTER 6: JAVA COLLECTIONS FRAMEWORK

30 Multiple Choice Questions (MCQs) :

---

1. Which of the following is not part of the Java Collections Framework?

a) List
b) Set
c) Map
d) Array

Answer: d) Array

---

2. Which of the following classes implements the List interface?

a) HashSet
b) TreeSet
c) LinkedList
d) PriorityQueue

Answer: c) LinkedList

---

3. Which method is used to add an element to a collection?

a) insert()
b) add()
c) append()
d) push()

Answer: b) add()

---

4. What does the size() method of a List return?

a) The sum of elements in the list
b) The number of elements in the list
c) The first element in the list
d) The last element in the list

Answer: b) The number of elements in the list

---

5. Which collection type allows only unique elements?

a) List
b) Set
c) Map
d) Queue

Answer: b) Set

---

6. Which class implements the Set interface?

a) HashMap
b) LinkedHashSet
c) TreeMap
d) Vector

Answer: b) LinkedHashSet

---

7. Which of the following classes implements the Map interface?

a) TreeSet
b) HashSet
c) LinkedList
d) HashMap

Answer: d) HashMap

---

8. What is the default initial capacity of a HashMap?

a) 10
b) 5
c) 16
d) 20

Answer: c) 16

9. Which method is used to remove an element from a List?

a) delete()
b) remove()
c) pop()
d) deleteElement()

Answer: b) remove()

---

10. Which collection class is ordered but does not allow duplicate elements?

a) LinkedHashSet
b) HashSet
c) PriorityQueue
d) ArrayList

Answer: a) LinkedHashSet

---

11. Which of the following is not a part of the Java Collections Framework?

a) PriorityQueue
b) LinkedHashMap
c) Stack
d) TreeSet

Answer: c) Stack

---

12. Which of the following interfaces does NOT extend Collection?

a) List
b) Set
c) Queue
d) Map

Answer: d) Map

---

13. Which of the following collection types uses a priority queue?

a) TreeSet
b) PriorityQueue
c) LinkedHashMap
d) HashSet

Answer: b) PriorityQueue

---

14. Which of the following collections does not maintain the insertion order?

a) LinkedList
b) ArrayList
c) HashSet
d) LinkedHashSet

Answer: c) HashSet

---

15. What will happen if you try to add a duplicate element to a Set?

a) It will replace the existing element.
b) It will throw an exception.
c) It will not add the element.
d) It will return false.

Answer: c) It will not add the element.

---

16. Which of the following classes is not a direct subclass of the AbstractList class?

a) ArrayList
b) LinkedList
c) Vector
d) HashSet

Answer: d) HashSet

---

17. Which interface does not extend Collection?

a) List
b) Set
c) Queue
d) Map

Answer: d) Map

---

18. Which of the following is true about the LinkedList class?

a) It is a part of the Set interface.
b) It is a doubly linked list.
c) It allows only unique elements.
d) It implements the Map interface.

Answer: b) It is a doubly linked list.

---

19. Which method is used to obtain an element from a List?

a) get()
b) retrieve()
c) fetch()
d) fetchElement()

Answer: a) get()

---

20. Which of the following is a valid method to iterate through the elements of a Set in Java?

a) forEach()
b) listIterator()
c) iterator()
d) all of the above

Answer: c) iterator()

---

21. Which of the following is NOT true about the Java Collections Framework?

a) It provides a set of interfaces and classes to handle collections of objects.
b) It is used to store objects in a systematic manner.
c) It only works with primitive data types.
d) It includes classes for sorting, searching, and synchronizing data.

Answer: c) It only works with primitive data types.

---

22. Which method is used to check whether a collection is empty or not?

a) isEmpty()
b) isFull()
c) isExist()
d) checkEmpty()

Answer: a) isEmpty()

---

23. Which of the following collections does not allow duplicate elements?

a) List
b) Set
c) Queue
d) Map

Answer: b) Set

---

24. Which of the following classes implements the Queue interface?

a) LinkedHashSet
b) TreeMap
c) LinkedList
d) ArrayList

Answer: c) LinkedList

---

25. What is the main difference between a HashMap and a TreeMap?

a) TreeMap is slower than HashMap.
b) HashMap is ordered while TreeMap is unordered.

c) HashMap maintains insertion order, while TreeMap sorts the keys.
d) TreeMap can store null values, while HashMap cannot.

Answer: c) HashMap maintains insertion order, while TreeMap sorts the keys.

---

26. Which collection class is best for implementing a stack?

a) LinkedList
b) PriorityQueue
c) HashMap
d) Vector

Answer: d) Vector

---

27. Which of the following methods is used to remove all elements from a collection?

a) clear()
b) removeAll()
c) deleteAll()
d) reset()

Answer: a) clear()

---

28. Which of the following interfaces does not extend Collection?

a) List
b) Set
c) Map
d) Queue

Answer: c) Map

---

29. Which of the following methods returns true if a collection contains a specific element?

a) has()
b) contains()
c) includes()
d) present()

Answer: b) contains()

---

30. Which of the following collections allows fast access to elements by index?

a) ArrayList
b) HashSet
c) TreeSet
d) LinkedList

Answer: a) ArrayList

30 Short Questions and Answers :

---

1. What is the Java Collections Framework?

Answer: The Java Collections Framework is a set of classes and interfaces that implement commonly used data structures like lists, sets, maps, and queues to store, retrieve, manipulate, and aggregate data.

---

2. What is the difference between a List and a Set?

Answer: A List allows duplicate elements and maintains insertion order, while a Set does not allow duplicates and does not guarantee order.

---

3. Which interface does a HashMap implement?

Answer: HashMap implements the **Map** interface.

---

4. What is the default initial capacity of an ArrayList in Java?

Answer: The default initial capacity of an ArrayList is **10**.

---

5. What is the difference between ArrayList and LinkedList?

Answer: ArrayList is backed by a dynamic array, while LinkedList is backed by a doubly linked list. LinkedList performs better for insertions and deletions, while ArrayList is faster for random access.

---

6. What is a HashSet?

Answer: HashSet is a collection that implements the **Set** interface, does not allow duplicate elements, and does not guarantee the order of elements.

---

7. What does the method `size()` return in a collection?

Answer: The `size()` method returns the number of elements in a collection.

---

8. What is the main use of a `Map` in Java?

Answer: A `Map` stores key-value pairs, allowing for fast lookups by key.

---

9. What is a TreeSet?

Answer: TreeSet is a collection that implements the **Set** interface and stores elements in a sorted order.

---

10. What does the `add()` method do in a collection?

Answer: The `add()` method adds an element to a collection. If the collection allows duplicates, the element is added, otherwise, it is ignored.

---

11. What is the purpose of the `clear()` method in collections?

Answer: The `clear()` method removes all elements from a collection.

---

12. What is the main difference between `HashMap` and `TreeMap`?

Answer: `HashMap` does not maintain any order, while `TreeMap` sorts the keys in ascending order by default.

---

13. Which interface does the `PriorityQueue` implement?

Answer: The `PriorityQueue` class implements the **Queue** interface.

---

14. What is the `contains()` method used for in collections?

Answer: The `contains()` method checks if a collection contains a specific element.

---

15. How can you iterate over a collection?

Answer: You can iterate over a collection using an **Iterator**, **for-each loop**, or a **Stream**.

---

16. What is the difference between `ArrayList` and `Vector`?

Answer: Both `ArrayList` and `Vector` are dynamic arrays, but `Vector` is synchronized, which makes it slower than `ArrayList`.

---

17. What is the purpose of `Collections.sort()` method?

Answer: The `Collections.sort()` method sorts the elements of a list in ascending order.

---

18. What is the function of the `poll()` method in a Queue?

Answer: The `poll()` method retrieves and removes the head of the queue, or returns `null` if the queue is empty.

---

19. What is a `LinkedHashMap`?

Answer: A `LinkedHashMap` is a hash map that maintains the order of insertion of keys.

---

20. What is the purpose of the `remove()` method in collections?

Answer: The `remove()` method removes a specified element from a collection.

---

21. What is the difference between `HashSet` and `LinkedHashSet`?

Answer: `HashSet` does not guarantee order, while `LinkedHashSet` maintains insertion order.

---

22. What is the function of the `addAll()` method?

Answer: The `addAll()` method adds all the elements from one collection to another.

---

23. What is a `Stack` in Java?

Answer: A `Stack` is a collection that represents a last-in, first-out (LIFO) data structure, where elements are added and removed from the top.

---

24. What is the difference between a `Map` and a `Set`?

Answer: A `Map` stores key-value pairs, whereas a `Set` stores only unique elements with no associated key.

---

25. How can you check if a collection is empty?

Answer: You can check if a collection is empty using the `isEmpty()` method.

26. What is the purpose of the `iterator()` method in collections?

Answer: The `iterator()` method returns an iterator that can be used to iterate over the elements of a collection.

27. What is the difference between `equals()` and `hashCode()` in collections?

Answer: `equals()` checks if two objects are equal, while `hashCode()` returns a hash value that is used for quick lookups in hash-based collections like `HashSet` and `HashMap`.

28. What is the use of `Collections.reverse()`?

Answer: The `Collections.reverse()` method reverses the order of elements in a list.

29. What does the `keySet()` method return in a Map?

Answer: The `keySet()` method returns a `Set` view of the keys in the map.

30. What is a `Vector` in Java?

Answer: A `Vector` is a resizable array implementation that implements the **List** interface and is synchronized, making it thread-safe but slower compared to other list implementations like `ArrayList`.

12 Practical Questions with Answers:

1. Write a program to create an ArrayList, add elements to it, and print the list.

Answer:

```
import java.util.ArrayList;
```

```
public class ArrayListExample {
    public static void main(String[] args) {
        // Create an ArrayList
        ArrayList<String> list = new ArrayList<>();

        // Add elements to the ArrayList
        list.add("Java");
        list.add("Python");
        list.add("C++");

        // Print the ArrayList
        System.out.println("ArrayList: " + list);
    }
}
```

Output:

```
ArrayList: [Java, Python, C++]
```

---

2. Write a program to create a HashSet, add elements, and check if an element exists in the HashSet.

Answer:

```
import java.util.HashSet;

public class HashSetExample {
    public static void main(String[] args) {
        // Create a HashSet
        HashSet<String> set = new HashSet<>();

        // Add elements to the HashSet
        set.add("Apple");
        set.add("Banana");
        set.add("Mango");

        // Check if an element exists in the set
        if(set.contains("Banana")) {
            System.out.println("Banana exists in the HashSet.");
        } else {
            System.out.println("Banana does not exist in the HashSet.");
        }
    }
}
```

Output:

```
arduino
Copy
Banana exists in the HashSet.
```

---

3. Write a program to demonstrate the use of TreeMap by adding some entries and printing them.

Answer:

```java
import java.util.TreeMap;

public class TreeMapExample {
    public static void main(String[] args) {
        // Create a TreeMap
        TreeMap<Integer, String> map = new TreeMap<>();

        // Add elements to the TreeMap
        map.put(1, "One");
        map.put(2, "Two");
        map.put(3, "Three");

        // Print the TreeMap
        System.out.println("TreeMap: " + map);
    }
}
```

Output:

```
TreeMap: {1=One, 2=Two, 3=Three}
```

4. Write a program to demonstrate how to remove an element from an ArrayList.

Answer:

```java
import java.util.ArrayList;

public class ArrayListRemoveExample {
    public static void main(String[] args) {
        // Create an ArrayList
        ArrayList<String> list = new ArrayList<>();

        // Add elements to the ArrayList
        list.add("Java");
        list.add("Python");
        list.add("C++");

        // Remove an element
        list.remove("Python");

        // Print the ArrayList after removal
        System.out.println("ArrayList after removal: " + list);
    }
}
```

Output:

```
ArrayList after removal: [Java, C++]
```

5. Write a program to iterate through a HashMap and print its key-value pairs.

Answer:

```java
import java.util.HashMap;

public class HashMapIterationExample {
    public static void main(String[] args) {
        // Create a HashMap
        HashMap<Integer, String> map = new HashMap<>();

        // Add elements to the HashMap
        map.put(1, "One");
        map.put(2, "Two");
        map.put(3, "Three");

        // Iterate and print the key-value pairs
        for (Map.Entry<Integer, String> entry : map.entrySet()) {
            System.out.println(entry.getKey() + ": " + entry.getValue());
        }
    }
}
```

Output:

```
1: One
2: Two
3: Three
```

6. Write a program to demonstrate how to use a LinkedList to add and remove elements.

Answer:

```java
import java.util.LinkedList;

public class LinkedListExample {
    public static void main(String[] args) {
        // Create a LinkedList
        LinkedList<String> list = new LinkedList<>();

        // Add elements to the LinkedList
        list.add("Java");
        list.add("Python");
        list.add("C++");
```

```java
        // Remove an element from the LinkedList
        list.remove("Python");

        // Print the LinkedList after removal
        System.out.println("LinkedList: " + list);
    }
}
```

Output:

```
LinkedList: [Java, C++]
```

7. Write a program to check if a HashSet is empty.

Answer:

```java
import java.util.HashSet;

public class HashSetEmptyCheck {
    public static void main(String[] args) {
        // Create a HashSet
        HashSet<String> set = new HashSet<>();

        // Check if the HashSet is empty
        if(set.isEmpty()) {
            System.out.println("The HashSet is empty.");
        } else {
            System.out.println("The HashSet is not empty.");
        }

        // Add an element
        set.add("Java");

        // Check again if the HashSet is empty
        if(set.isEmpty()) {
            System.out.println("The HashSet is empty.");
        } else {
            System.out.println("The HashSet is not empty.");
        }
    }
}
```

Output:

```
The HashSet is empty.
The HashSet is not empty.
```

8. Write a program to demonstrate the use of contains() method in a List.

Answer:

```java
import java.util.ArrayList;

public class ArrayListContainsExample {
    public static void main(String[] args) {
        // Create an ArrayList
        ArrayList<String> list = new ArrayList<>();

        // Add elements to the ArrayList
        list.add("Java");
        list.add("Python");
        list.add("C++");

        // Check if an element exists
        if(list.contains("Python")) {
            System.out.println("Python is in the list.");
        } else {
            System.out.println("Python is not in the list.");
        }
    }
}
```

Output:

```
Python is in the list.
```

---

9. Write a program to reverse a LinkedList.

Answer:

```java
import java.util.LinkedList;

public class LinkedListReverse {
    public static void main(String[] args) {
        // Create a LinkedList
        LinkedList<String> list = new LinkedList<>();

        // Add elements to the LinkedList
        list.add("Java");
        list.add("Python");
        list.add("C++");

        // Reverse the LinkedList
        LinkedList<String> reversedList = new LinkedList<>();
        for (int i = list.size() - 1; i >= 0; i--) {
            reversedList.add(list.get(i));
        }

        // Print the reversed LinkedList
        System.out.println("Reversed LinkedList: " + reversedList);
    }
}
```

Output:

Reversed LinkedList: [C++, Python, Java]

10. Write a program to sort an ArrayList in ascending order.

Answer:

```java
import java.util.ArrayList;
import java.util.Collections;

public class ArrayListSortExample {
    public static void main(String[] args) {
        // Create an ArrayList
        ArrayList<Integer> list = new ArrayList<>();

        // Add elements to the ArrayList
        list.add(10);
        list.add(30);
        list.add(20);

        // Sort the ArrayList
        Collections.sort(list);

        // Print the sorted ArrayList
        System.out.println("Sorted ArrayList: " + list);
    }
}
```

Output:

```
Sorted ArrayList: [10, 20, 30]
```

11. Write a program to check if two Lists are equal.

Answer:

```java
import java.util.ArrayList;

public class ListEqualityCheck {
    public static void main(String[] args) {
        // Create two ArrayLists
        ArrayList<String> list1 = new ArrayList<>();
        ArrayList<String> list2 = new ArrayList<>();

        // Add elements to both lists
        list1.add("Java");
        list1.add("Python");

        list2.add("Java");
        list2.add("Python");

        // Check if the lists are equal
```

```
        if(list1.equals(list2)) {
            System.out.println("The lists are equal.");
        } else {
            System.out.println("The lists are not equal.");
        }
    }
}
```

Output:

```
The lists are equal.
```

12. Write a program to remove all elements from a HashSet.

Answer:

```java
import java.util.HashSet;

public class HashSetClearExample {
    public static void main(String[] args) {
        // Create a HashSet
        HashSet<String> set = new HashSet<>();

        // Add elements to the HashSet
        set.add("Java");
        set.add("Python");
        set.add("C++");

        // Remove all elements
        set.clear();

        // Print the HashSet after clearing
        System.out.println("HashSet after clearing: " + set);
    }
}
```

Output:

```
HashSet after clearing: []
```

10 Long Answer Questions

1. Explain the Java Collections Framework. What are its major interfaces and classes?

Answer:

The **Java Collections Framework** is a set of classes and interfaces that implement commonly reusable collection data structures. It provides various classes and interfaces for storing and manipulating data in Java. The framework includes algorithms for sorting, searching, and manipulating data.

Major Interfaces in the Java Collections Framework:

1. **Collection Interface**: The root interface in the collection hierarchy, which defines the basic operations (add, remove, size, etc.) for all collections.
2. **List Interface**: A sub-interface of `Collection` that represents an ordered collection of elements. Examples: `ArrayList`, `LinkedList`.
3. **Set Interface**: A collection that does not allow duplicate elements. Examples: `HashSet`, `TreeSet`.
4. **Queue Interface**: A collection designed for holding elements in a particular order, often in a FIFO (First In First Out) manner. Examples: `PriorityQueue`, `LinkedList`.
5. **Map Interface**: Unlike other collections, `Map` holds key-value pairs. It allows for quick lookups by key. Examples: `HashMap`, `TreeMap`, `LinkedHashMap`.

Major Classes in the Java Collections Framework:

1. **ArrayList**: A resizable array that implements the `List` interface. It allows duplicate elements and maintains insertion order.
2. **LinkedList**: A doubly linked list implementation of the `List` interface. It supports fast insertions and deletions.
3. **HashSet**: An implementation of the `Set` interface backed by a hash table. It does not allow duplicate elements and does not guarantee any order.
4. **TreeSet**: A `Set` implementation based on a tree structure. It maintains elements in a sorted order.
5. **HashMap**: Implements the `Map` interface using a hash table. It allows key-value mappings and ensures quick retrieval of values by their keys.
6. **TreeMap**: Implements the `Map` interface using a red-black tree structure, keeping keys in sorted order.

---

2. What is the difference between ArrayList and LinkedList? Compare their performance.

Answer:

Both **ArrayList** and **LinkedList** implement the `List` interface in Java but have different internal structures, leading to performance differences in various operations.

*   **ArrayList:**

- o **Internal Structure**: It uses a dynamic array to store elements.
- o **Access Time**: ArrayList offers constant time (`O(1)`) for random access because it uses an array.
- o **Insertion/Deletion**: Insertions and deletions in the middle of the list take linear time (`O(n)`) as it requires shifting elements.
- o **Memory Usage**: ArrayList consumes less memory as it stores elements in a contiguous block of memory.
- **LinkedList**:
  - o **Internal Structure**: It uses a doubly linked list where each element points to the next and previous elements.
  - o **Access Time**: Accessing an element takes linear time (`O(n)`) as it requires traversal through the list.
  - o **Insertion/Deletion**: Insertions and deletions at both ends (head/tail) take constant time (`O(1)`), but in the middle of the list, it requires traversal to the desired position, which is linear time (`O(n)`).
  - o **Memory Usage**: LinkedList requires more memory as each element needs extra space for pointers to the next and previous elements.

Performance Comparison:

- ArrayList is generally faster for random access (i.e., retrieving an element by index) and works best when elements are added at the end of the list.
- LinkedList is more efficient when frequent insertions or deletions are required, especially at the beginning or middle of the list.

---

3. What is a HashMap in Java? Explain how it works and its basic operations.

Answer:

HashMap is part of the Java Collections Framework and implements the `Map` interface. It stores key-value pairs and provides fast access to values using keys. It is backed by a hash table, where the keys are hashed to find the corresponding value.

How HashMap Works:

- **Hashing**: Each key in a HashMap is hashed using its `hashCode()` method, which returns an integer value. This hash is then used to calculate the index in the internal array where the key-value pair will be stored.
- **Bucket**: The array used by HashMap is divided into "buckets," and each bucket can hold one or more key-value pairs (when collisions occur).
- **Collision Handling**: When two keys hash to the same index (i.e., collision), HashMap uses a linked list or tree structure within the bucket to store multiple key-value pairs.

- **Load Factor**: HashMap has an initial capacity and a load factor. The load factor determines when the map should resize. When the map reaches a threshold (capacity * load factor), it resizes to accommodate more entries.

Basic Operations:

1. **put(key, value)**: Adds a key-value pair to the map.
2. **get(key)**: Retrieves the value associated with the given key.
3. **remove(key)**: Removes the key-value pair with the specified key.
4. **containsKey(key)**: Checks if a key exists in the map.
5. **size()**: Returns the number of key-value pairs in the map.
6. **clear()**: Removes all key-value pairs from the map.

Example:

```java
import java.util.HashMap;

public class HashMapExample {
    public static void main(String[] args) {
        HashMap<Integer, String> map = new HashMap<>();

        map.put(1, "One");
        map.put(2, "Two");
        map.put(3, "Three");

        System.out.println(map.get(2));   // Output: Two
    }
}
```

---

4. What is the difference between HashMap and TreeMap?

Answer:

Both **HashMap** and **TreeMap** are implementations of the Map interface in Java, but they differ in their internal structures and behavior.

HashMap:

- **Internal Structure**: HashMap uses a hash table to store key-value pairs.
- **Order**: HashMap does not guarantee any order of its elements. The order of the entries is determined by the hash function and is not predictable.
- **Performance**: HashMap provides constant time complexity ($O(1)$) for basic operations like put(), get(), and remove() when the hash function distributes elements evenly. In the worst case, it can degrade to linear time ($O(n)$).
- **Null Values**: HashMap allows null as a key or value.
- **Example**: HashMap<Integer, String> map = new HashMap<>();

TreeMap:

- **Internal Structure**: TreeMap is implemented using a red-black tree (a self-balancing binary search tree).
- **Order**: TreeMap maintains its elements in a sorted order based on the natural ordering of the keys or a specified comparator.
- **Performance**: TreeMap provides `O(log n)` time complexity for basic operations like `put()`, `get()`, and `remove()` due to the tree structure.
- **Null Values**: TreeMap does not allow `null` keys but allows `null` values.
- **Example**: `TreeMap<Integer, String> map = new TreeMap<>();`

Summary:

- Use `HashMap` when you do not require any ordering of the elements and need faster performance.
- Use `TreeMap` when you need the elements to be stored in a sorted order (either natural order or custom order).

---

5. Explain the difference between a List and a Set in Java.

Answer:

In Java, both **List** and **Set** are collections that store elements, but they have key differences in how they handle the elements:

List:

- A **List** is an ordered collection that allows duplicate elements.
- It maintains the order in which elements are inserted (i.e., it is index-based).
- Common implementations of List include `ArrayList`, `LinkedList`, and `Vector`.
- Elements can be accessed by their index position, and you can have multiple occurrences of the same element.

Set:

- A **Set** is an unordered collection that does not allow duplicate elements.
- It does not maintain the order of elements.
- Common implementations of Set include `HashSet`, `LinkedHashSet`, and `TreeSet`.
- Sets do not allow duplicate elements, so if you try to add a duplicate, it will be ignored.

Key Differences:

- **Order**: Lists maintain the insertion order, whereas Sets do not guarantee order (though `LinkedHashSet` and `TreeSet` have specific ordering mechanisms).

- **Duplicates**: Lists allow duplicates, while Sets do not allow duplicate elements.
- **Access**: In Lists, elements are accessed by index, while in Sets, there is no index-based access.

6. What is the difference between ArrayList and Vector?

Answer:

Both **ArrayList** and **Vector** are implementations of the `List` interface, but they have key differences:

ArrayList:

- **Synchronization**: ArrayList is **not synchronized**, meaning it is not thread-safe.
- **Performance**: Because it is not synchronized, ArrayList generally performs better than Vector when multiple threads are not involved.
- **Growth Factor**: ArrayList grows dynamically as elements are added. By default, it grows by 50% of its size when more space is needed.
- **Use Case**: ArrayList is typically preferred in most situations where thread-safety is not a concern.

Vector:

- **Synchronization**: Vector is **synchronized**, making it thread-safe for concurrent use by multiple threads.
- **Performance**: Due to synchronization, Vector can be slower than ArrayList when there is no need for thread safety.
- **Growth Factor**: Vector grows by doubling its size when it runs out of space, which can sometimes result in wasted memory.
- **Use Case**: Vector is used when thread safety is required, but it is generally recommended to use `ArrayList` and `Collections.synchronizedList()` for thread safety instead of `Vector`.

7. Explain the use of the Iterator interface in Java.

Answer:

The **Iterator** interface is part of the `java.util` package and is used to iterate over collections (like List, Set, etc.) in a standardized way. It provides methods to traverse through elements of a collection, without exposing the underlying structure.

Methods in Iterator Interface:

1. **hasNext()**: Returns `true` if there are more elements to iterate, `false` otherwise.
2. **next()**: Returns the next element in the iteration.
3. **remove()**: Removes the last element returned by the iterator. This method is optional.

Example:

```java
import java.util.ArrayList;
import java.util.Iterator;

public class IteratorExample {
    public static void main(String[] args) {
        ArrayList<String> list = new ArrayList<>();
        list.add("Java");
        list.add("Python");
        list.add("C++");

        Iterator<String> iterator = list.iterator();

        while(iterator.hasNext()) {
            System.out.println(iterator.next());
        }
    }
}
```

8. Explain the concept of Generics in Java Collections.

Answer:

Generics in Java allow you to specify the type of objects that can be stored in a collection. It ensures type safety, meaning the compiler will check the type of objects at compile time, preventing `ClassCastException` at runtime.

Benefits of Generics:

1. **Type Safety**: Generics allow you to define a collection that can hold only objects of a specific type, ensuring compile-time type checking.
2. **Eliminates Casts**: When you use generics, you do not need to cast objects when retrieving them from a collection, as the collection is already typed.
3. **Code Reusability**: Generics allow you to create classes, interfaces, and methods that work with any object type.

Example:

```java
import java.util.ArrayList;

public class GenericExample {
    public static void main(String[] args) {
        // Create a generic ArrayList of Strings
        ArrayList<String> list = new ArrayList<>();
```

```
        list.add("Java");
        list.add("Python");

        // No need to cast when retrieving elements
        String element = list.get(0);
        System.out.println(element);  // Output: Java
    }
}
```

9. What is a PriorityQueue in Java and how is it different from a regular Queue?

Answer:

A **PriorityQueue** is a special kind of queue where elements are ordered according to their natural ordering or by a comparator provided at the time of creation. Unlike a regular queue, which follows **FIFO (First In First Out)**, a **PriorityQueue** uses the priority of elements for their retrieval.

Key Differences between PriorityQueue and Regular Queue:

- **Order**: In a regular queue, elements are processed in the order they are added (FIFO). In a PriorityQueue, elements are processed based on their priority (i.e., smallest or largest, depending on the comparator).
- **Access**: In a regular queue, elements are accessed in the order they are added. In a PriorityQueue, elements are accessed in the order determined by their priority.

Example:

```
import java.util.PriorityQueue;

public class PriorityQueueExample {
    public static void main(String[] args) {
        PriorityQueue<Integer> pq = new PriorityQueue<>();
        pq.add(10);
        pq.add(5);
        pq.add(20);

        // Elements will be retrieved in order of priority (smallest first)
        System.out.println(pq.poll());  // Output: 5
    }
}
```

9. What are some of the important methods provided by the Collections class in Java?

Answer:

The **Collections** class in Java provides static methods for operating on or returning collections. It contains various utility methods for sorting, searching, and manipulating collections.

Important Methods in Collections Class:

1. **sort(List<T> list)**: Sorts the specified list into ascending order.
2. **reverse(List<T> list)**: Reverses the order of elements in the list.
3. **shuffle(List<T> list)**: Randomly permutes the elements in the list.
4. **min(Collection<T> coll)**: Returns the minimum element in the collection according to its natural ordering or a comparator.
5. **max(Collection<T> coll)**: Returns the maximum element in the collection according to its natural ordering or a comparator.
6. **frequency(Collection<T> coll, Object o)**: Returns the number of occurrences of the specified element in the collection.
7. **copy(List<? super T> dest, List<? extends T> src)**: Copies all elements from the source list to the destination list.
8. **singletonList(T o)**: Returns an immutable list containing only the specified element.
9. **unmodifiableList(List<? extends T> list)**: Returns an unmodifiable view of the specified list.

CHAPTER 7: JAVA FILE HANDLING

30 multiple-choice questions (MCQs):

---

1. What is the root class for all file-based operations in Java?

a) FileReader
b) File
c) BufferedReader
d) FileInputStream

Answer: b) File

---

2. Which of the following classes is used to read the contents of a file?

a) FileOutputStream
b) FileReader
c) FileWriter
d) BufferedWriter

Answer: b) FileReader

---

3. What method is used to create a new file in Java?

a) createFile()
b) createNewFile()
c) newFile()
d) newFileMethod()

Answer: b) createNewFile()

---

4. Which of the following classes is used for reading character files?

a) FileReader
b) FileInputStream
c) DataInputStream
d) BufferedOutputStream

Answer: a) FileReader

---

5. What is the default character encoding used by FileReader in Java?

a) UTF-8
b) ASCII
c) UTF-16
d) System default encoding

Answer: d) System default encoding

---

6. Which class is used to write data to a file in Java?

a) FileWriter
b) FileReader
c) FileOutputStream
d) File

Answer: a) FileWriter

---

7. Which method is used to delete a file in Java?

a) deleteFile()
b) delete()
c) remove()
d) deleteFileMethod()

Answer: b) delete()

---

8. Which class can be used to buffer data in Java file handling to improve performance?

a) BufferedReader
b) BufferedWriter
c) BufferedStream
d) All of the above

Answer: d) All of the above

---

9. What method is used to check whether a file exists in Java?

a) exists()
b) isFile()
c) checkExists()
d) validate()

Answer: a) exists()

---

10. Which of the following is the correct way to close a file stream in Java?

a) closeStream()
b) close()
c) end()
d) stop()

Answer: b) close()

---

11. What is the default buffer size for BufferedReader in Java?

a) 128 bytes
b) 512 bytes
c) 1024 bytes
d) 8192 bytes

Answer: d) 8192 bytes

---

12. Which class is used to read binary data from a file?

a) FileReader
b) BufferedReader
c) FileInputStream
d) ObjectInputStream

Answer: c) FileInputStream

13. Which method is used to read a line of text from a file using BufferedReader?

a) read()
b) readLine()
c) readChar()
d) readText()

Answer: b) readLine()

14. Which class is used to read both text and binary data from a file?

a) FileReader
b) FileWriter
c) RandomAccessFile
d) FileInputStream

Answer: c) RandomAccessFile

15. Which of the following methods is used to write data to a file using FileWriter?

a) writeData()
b) writeToFile()
c) write()
d) append()

Answer: c) write()

16. Which method of File class is used to rename a file?

a) renameFile()
b) renameTo()
c) changeName()
d) modifyName()

Answer: b) renameTo()

17. Which of the following classes is used to read a file in a system-independent way?

a) File
b) FileReader
c) FileInputStream
d) Path

Answer: d) Path

18. Which method of the File class is used to get the length of a file?

a) getFileLength()
b) getSize()
c) length()
d) fileSize()

Answer: c) length()

19. What type of exception is thrown if an error occurs during file handling in Java?

a) FileNotFoundException
b) IOException
c) FileHandlingException
d) Both a and b

Answer: d) Both a and b

20. What does the method getAbsolutePath() of the File class return?

a) The file path relative to the current working directory
b) The file's absolute location
c) The path to the file's parent directory
d) The name of the file

Answer: b) The file's absolute location

21. What method is used to write the content to a file in Java using BufferedWriter?

a) writeText()
b) append()
c) write()
d) print()

Answer: c) write()

22. Which of the following is true about FileInputStream?

a) It is used for reading binary data from a file
b) It is used for reading character data from a file
c) It is used for writing binary data to a file
d) It is used for writing character data to a file

Answer: a) It is used for reading binary data from a file

23. Which method is used to get the name of the file in Java?

a) getName()
b) getFileName()
c) fileName()
d) retrieveName()

Answer: a) getName()

24. What is the correct way to copy content from one file to another?

a) Using FileInputStream and FileOutputStream
b) Using BufferedReader and BufferedWriter
c) Using both FileInputStream and FileOutputStream
d) Both a and b

Answer: d) Both a and b

25. What does the FileWriter append() method do?

a) It writes data to a file
b) It reads data from a file
c) It appends data to the end of a file
d) It removes data from a file

Answer: c) It appends data to the end of a file

---

26. How would you ensure that a file is properly closed after reading or writing data?

a) By using try-catch blocks
b) By using the close() method explicitly
c) By using try-with-resources (automatic closing)
d) By using finalize()

Answer: c) By using try-with-resources (automatic closing)

---

27. Which of the following methods is used to create directories in Java?

a) mkdir()
b) makeDirectory()
c) createDirectory()
d) createNewDirectory()

Answer: a) mkdir()

---

28. What is the use of the RandomAccessFile class in Java?

a) To read from and write to a file at any position
b) To read data sequentially from a file
c) To write data to a file
d) To append data to a file

Answer: a) To read from and write to a file at any position

---

29. How do you handle IO exceptions when working with files in Java?

a) By using throw keyword
b) By using try-catch blocks
c) By using throws keyword
d) Both b and c

Answer: d) Both b and c

---

30. Which method is used to check if a file is a directory?

a) isFile()
b) isDirectory()
c) checkDirectory()
d) validateDirectory()

Answer: b) isDirectory()

30 short questions with answers:

---

1. What is the purpose of the File class in Java?

Answer: The File class represents files and directory pathnames in an abstract manner. It is used to create, delete, and manipulate files and directories.

---

2. Which class is used to read data from a file in Java?

Answer: The `FileReader` class is used to read data from a file in Java.

---

3. Which class is used for reading binary data in Java?

Answer: The `FileInputStream` class is used for reading binary data from a file.

---

4. How do you check if a file exists in Java?

Answer: You can use the `exists()` method of the `File` class to check if a file exists.

---

5. What does the `createNewFile()` method do in Java?

Answer: The `createNewFile()` method creates a new empty file if it does not already exist. It returns `true` if the file is created successfully and `false` if the file already exists.

---

6. How do you delete a file in Java?

Answer: You can delete a file using the `delete()` method of the `File` class.

---

7. What is the purpose of the `FileWriter` class in Java?

Answer: The `FileWriter` class is used to write character data to a file.

---

8. What is the use of the `BufferedReader` class?

Answer: The `BufferedReader` class is used to read text from a file efficiently, providing a buffering mechanism for reading characters, arrays, and lines.

---

9. How do you append data to an existing file in Java?

Answer: To append data, create a `FileWriter` object with the second argument as `true` (e.g., `FileWriter writer = new FileWriter("file.txt", true);`).

---

10. Which method is used to read a line from a file using `BufferedReader`?

Answer: The `readLine()` method is used to read a line of text from a file using `BufferedReader`.

---

11. What method in the `File` class checks if a file is a directory?

Answer: The `isDirectory()` method checks if a file is a directory.

---

12. How do you get the length of a file in Java?

Answer: You can use the `length()` method of the `File` class to get the length of a file in bytes.

---

13. Which exception is thrown when a file is not found in Java?

Answer: The `FileNotFoundException` is thrown when a file cannot be found.

---

14. What is the function of the `FileInputStream` class?

Answer: The `FileInputStream` class is used to read raw byte data from a file.

---

15. How do you get the absolute path of a file in Java?

Answer: The `getAbsolutePath()` method returns the absolute path of a file.

---

16. What does the `mkdir()` method do in Java?

Answer: The `mkdir()` method is used to create a new directory in the file system.

---

17. How do you rename a file in Java?

Answer: You can rename a file using the `renameTo()` method of the `File` class.

---

18. What is the purpose of the `FileOutputStream` class?

Answer: The `FileOutputStream` class is used to write binary data to a file.

---

19. What does the `delete()` method do in the `File` class?

Answer: The `delete()` method deletes the file or directory represented by the `File` object.

20. How do you get the name of a file in Java?

Answer: You can use the `getName()` method of the `File` class to get the name of a file.

21. What is the function of the `RandomAccessFile` class?

Answer: The `RandomAccessFile` class allows reading and writing to a file at any position, enabling random access to file content.

22. How can you create a file using Java?

Answer: You can create a file using the `createNewFile()` method of the `File` class.

23. What is the purpose of the `BufferedWriter` class in Java?

Answer: The `BufferedWriter` class is used to write text to a file efficiently by buffering characters.

24. What does the `FileReader` class do in Java?

Answer: The `FileReader` class is used for reading character-based data from a file.

25. How do you check if a file is readable or writable in Java?

Answer: You can use the `canRead()` and `canWrite()` methods of the `File` class to check if a file is readable or writable.

26. What is the difference between `FileInputStream` and `FileReader`?

Answer: `FileInputStream` is used for reading binary data, while `FileReader` is used for reading character data from a file.

---

27. Which class in Java is used to write data to a file byte by byte?

Answer: The `FileOutputStream` class is used to write data to a file byte by byte.

---

28. What is the `length()` method of the `File` class used for?

Answer: The `length()` method returns the size of the file in bytes.

---

29. What exception is thrown when there is an issue in reading a file?

Answer: An `IOException` is thrown when there is an issue while reading a file.

---

30. How do you copy a file in Java?

Answer: You can copy a file by using `FileInputStream` to read from the source file and `FileOutputStream` to write to the destination file.

10 practical questions with answers:

---

1. Practical Question: Write a program to create a new file named `testfile.txt` and write some text into it.

Answer:

```
import java.io.File;
import java.io.FileWriter;
import java.io.IOException;

public class CreateFileExample {
    public static void main(String[] args) {
        try {
```

```java
        File file = new File("testfile.txt");
        if (file.createNewFile()) {
            System.out.println("File created: " + file.getName());
        } else {
            System.out.println("File already exists.");
        }

        FileWriter writer = new FileWriter("testfile.txt");
        writer.write("Hello, this is a sample text.");
        writer.close();
        System.out.println("Successfully wrote to the file.");
    } catch (IOException e) {
        System.out.println("An error occurred.");
        e.printStackTrace();
    }
    }
}
```

2. Practical Question: Write a program to read the contents of `testfile.txt` and print it on the console.

Answer:

```java
import java.io.File;
import java.io.FileReader;
import java.io.BufferedReader;
import java.io.IOException;

public class ReadFileExample {
    public static void main(String[] args) {
        try {
            FileReader fr = new FileReader("testfile.txt");
            BufferedReader br = new BufferedReader(fr);
            String line;
            while ((line = br.readLine()) != null) {
                System.out.println(line);
            }
            br.close();
        } catch (IOException e) {
            System.out.println("An error occurred.");
            e.printStackTrace();
        }
    }
}
```

3. Practical Question: Write a program to check if a file `testfile.txt` exists and if so, print its length.

Answer:

```java
import java.io.File;
```

```
public class FileExistsAndLength {
    public static void main(String[] args) {
        File file = new File("testfile.txt");

        if (file.exists()) {
            System.out.println("File exists. File length: " + file.length() +
" bytes.");
        } else {
            System.out.println("File does not exist.");
        }
    }
}
```

4. Practical Question: Write a program to delete `testfile.txt` if it exists.

Answer:

```
import java.io.File;

public class DeleteFileExample {
    public static void main(String[] args) {
        File file = new File("testfile.txt");

        if (file.exists()) {
            if (file.delete()) {
                System.out.println("Deleted the file: " + file.getName());
            } else {
                System.out.println("Failed to delete the file.");
            }
        } else {
            System.out.println("File does not exist.");
        }
    }
}
```

5. Practical Question: Write a program to append a line of text to an existing file `testfile.txt`.

Answer:

```
import java.io.FileWriter;
import java.io.IOException;

public class AppendToFileExample {
    public static void main(String[] args) {
        try {
            FileWriter writer = new FileWriter("testfile.txt", true);
            writer.write("\nThis line is appended to the file.");
            writer.close();
            System.out.println("Successfully appended to the file.");
```

```
        } catch (IOException e) {
            System.out.println("An error occurred.");
            e.printStackTrace();
        }
    }
}
```

6. Practical Question: Write a program to rename a file `oldfile.txt` to `newfile.txt`.

Answer:

```
import java.io.File;

public class RenameFileExample {
    public static void main(String[] args) {
        File oldFile = new File("oldfile.txt");
        File newFile = new File("newfile.txt");

        if (oldFile.exists()) {
            if (oldFile.renameTo(newFile)) {
                System.out.println("File renamed successfully.");
            } else {
                System.out.println("File renaming failed.");
            }
        } else {
            System.out.println("File does not exist.");
        }
    }
}
```

7. Practical Question: Write a program to copy the contents of `source.txt` to `destination.txt`.

Answer:

```
import java.io.FileInputStream;
import java.io.FileOutputStream;
import java.io.IOException;

public class CopyFileExample {
    public static void main(String[] args) {
        try {
            FileInputStream source = new FileInputStream("source.txt");
            FileOutputStream destination = new
FileOutputStream("destination.txt");

            int byteRead;
            while ((byteRead = source.read()) != -1) {
                destination.write(byteRead);
            }
```

```java
            source.close();
            destination.close();
            System.out.println("File copied successfully.");
        } catch (IOException e) {
            System.out.println("An error occurred.");
            e.printStackTrace();
        }
    }
}
```

8. Practical Question: Write a program to display the name of all files in the current directory.

Answer:

```java
import java.io.File;

public class ListFilesInDirectory {
    public static void main(String[] args) {
        File directory = new File(".");

        if (directory.exists() && directory.isDirectory()) {
            String[] files = directory.list();
            for (String fileName : files) {
                System.out.println(fileName);
            }
        } else {
            System.out.println("No files found or invalid directory.");
        }
    }
}
```

9. Practical Question: Write a program to create a directory `newDir` and a file `fileInNewDir.txt` inside that directory.

Answer:

```java
import java.io.File;
import java.io.FileWriter;
import java.io.IOException;

public class CreateDirectoryAndFile {
    public static void main(String[] args) {
        File dir = new File("newDir");

        if (dir.mkdir()) {
            System.out.println("Directory created: " + dir.getName());

            try {
                File file = new File("newDir/fileInNewDir.txt");
                if (file.createNewFile()) {
```

```
                    System.out.println("File created: " + file.getName());
                    FileWriter writer = new FileWriter(file);
                    writer.write("This is a file inside a new directory.");
                    writer.close();
                } else {
                    System.out.println("File already exists.");
                }
            } catch (IOException e) {
                System.out.println("An error occurred while creating the
file.");
            }
        } else {
            System.out.println("Directory already exists or could not be
created.");
        }
    }
}
```

10. Practical Question: Write a program to check if a file is readable and writable.

Answer:

```
import java.io.File;

public class CheckFilePermissions {
    public static void main(String[] args) {
        File file = new File("testfile.txt");

        if (file.exists()) {
            System.out.println("File is readable: " + file.canRead());
            System.out.println("File is writable: " + file.canWrite());
        } else {
            System.out.println("File does not exist.");
        }
    }
}
```

10 long-answer questions:

1. Question: Explain the process of reading from a file in Java. What are the classes and methods used for reading data from a file? Provide an example program.

Answer:
In Java, to read data from a file, we use classes from the `java.io` package such as `FileReader`, `BufferedReader`, `FileInputStream`, and `Scanner`. The most common approach for reading

files in Java is using the `BufferedReader` class, which reads text from a character-based input stream, buffering characters for efficient reading of characters, arrays, and lines.

Classes and Methods:

1. **FileReader**: This class is used to read the content of a file. It reads the file byte by byte.
2. **BufferedReader**: It is used to read data efficiently, buffering input for better performance. It has the method `readLine()` for reading the content line by line.
3. **FileInputStream**: This class reads binary data from a file, commonly used for reading non-text files (like images or audio files).
4. **Scanner**: This is a utility class used to read from files, among other things, and can parse different types of input.

Example:

```java
import java.io.FileReader;
import java.io.BufferedReader;
import java.io.IOException;

public class ReadFileExample {
    public static void main(String[] args) {
        try {
            FileReader fileReader = new FileReader("example.txt");
            BufferedReader bufferedReader = new BufferedReader(fileReader);

            String line;
            while ((line = bufferedReader.readLine()) != null) {
                System.out.println(line);
            }
            bufferedReader.close();
        } catch (IOException e) {
            System.out.println("An error occurred while reading the file.");
            e.printStackTrace();
        }
    }
}
```

In the above example:

- The file `example.txt` is opened using `FileReader`.
- `BufferedReader` is used to read the file line by line.
- The `readLine()` method reads the file content until the end of the file (EOF) is reached.

---

2. Question: What is file writing in Java? How does one write data to a file using Java? Explain different classes involved in writing data to a file.

Answer:
File writing in Java refers to the process of storing data into files. There are several classes in

Java that allow for writing to files, each suited for different types of writing operations. The most commonly used classes are `FileWriter`, `BufferedWriter`, `PrintWriter`, and `FileOutputStream`.

Classes Used for Writing Data:

1. **FileWriter**: This class writes character data to a file. It is typically used for writing text data and is often used in conjunction with `BufferedWriter` for efficient writing.
2. **BufferedWriter**: This class writes text to a file in an efficient manner by buffering characters before writing them. It has the `write()` and `newLine()` methods.
3. **PrintWriter**: This is an easy-to-use class for writing formatted text to a file. It is similar to `BufferedWriter` but with additional methods for printing formatted data.
4. **FileOutputStream**: This class writes binary data to a file. It is commonly used for writing non-text data such as images or audio files.

Example using FileWriter and BufferedWriter:

```java
import java.io.FileWriter;
import java.io.BufferedWriter;
import java.io.IOException;

public class WriteFileExample {
    public static void main(String[] args) {
        try {
            FileWriter fileWriter = new FileWriter("output.txt");
            BufferedWriter bufferedWriter = new BufferedWriter(fileWriter);

            bufferedWriter.write("This is an example of writing to a file in Java.");
            bufferedWriter.newLine();
            bufferedWriter.write("Java File I/O operations are very efficient.");

            bufferedWriter.close();
            System.out.println("Successfully wrote to the file.");
        } catch (IOException e) {
            System.out.println("An error occurred.");
            e.printStackTrace();
        }
    }
}
```

In this example:

- A file `output.txt` is created (or overwritten) using `FileWriter`.
- `BufferedWriter` is used to write lines of text to the file.
- The `newLine()` method inserts a new line after each write operation.

3. Question: How does file handling in Java differ between binary and text files? What classes are used for each type?

Answer:
In Java, file handling differs for **binary files** and **text files** based on the type of data that needs to be written or read.

1. **Text Files**:
    o   Text files store data as readable characters, typically in ASCII or UTF-8 encoding.
    o   For handling text files in Java, classes such as `FileReader`, `BufferedReader`, `FileWriter`, and `BufferedWriter` are used.
    o   These classes deal with characters and lines of text.
2. **Binary Files**:
    o   Binary files store data in the form of bytes. These files could be images, audio, video, or any file that is not meant to be human-readable.
    o   For binary files, `FileInputStream` and `FileOutputStream` are commonly used. These classes read and write raw bytes instead of characters.

Classes for Handling Text Files:

*   `FileReader` / `BufferedReader` (For reading text)
*   `FileWriter` / `BufferedWriter` (For writing text)

Classes for Handling Binary Files:

*   `FileInputStream` (For reading bytes)
*   `FileOutputStream` (For writing bytes)

Example of Reading Binary Data:

```
import java.io.FileInputStream;
import java.io.IOException;

public class ReadBinaryFile {
    public static void main(String[] args) {
        try {
            FileInputStream fis = new FileInputStream("image.jpg");
            int byteData;
            while ((byteData = fis.read()) != -1) {
                System.out.print((char) byteData); // Displaying the byte as
a character
            }
            fis.close();
        } catch (IOException e) {
            System.out.println("An error occurred while reading the binary
file.");
        }
    }
}
```

In this case, the file `image.jpg` is read byte by byte.

4. Question: Describe how to append data to a file in Java. What is the significance of the `true` parameter in the `FileWriter` constructor?

Answer:
In Java, to append data to a file, the `FileWriter` constructor has a boolean parameter that indicates whether the data should be appended to the file or overwrite it. By default, this parameter is set to `false`, meaning that the file will be overwritten if it already exists.

When the parameter is set to `true`, data is appended to the file instead of replacing the existing content. This is useful when we need to add new data without modifying the existing content.

Example of Appending Data:

```
import java.io.FileWriter;
import java.io.IOException;

public class AppendToFileExample {
    public static void main(String[] args) {
        try {
            FileWriter writer = new FileWriter("output.txt", true); // 'true'
enables appending
            writer.write("\nThis line is appended.");
            writer.close();
            System.out.println("Successfully appended to the file.");
        } catch (IOException e) {
            System.out.println("An error occurred.");
            e.printStackTrace();
        }
    }
}
```

In this example:

- The `FileWriter` is initialized with the `true` argument, meaning the text will be appended to `output.txt` rather than overwriting it.

5. Question: What are the various methods available in the `File` class for file manipulation in Java?

Answer:
The `File` class in Java is part of the `java.io` package and provides several methods for performing file-related operations, such as creating, deleting, renaming, and checking file properties. Some of the key methods are:

1. **createNewFile()**: Creates a new file if it doesn't already exist.

2. **delete()**: Deletes a file or directory.
3. **exists()**: Checks if a file or directory exists.
4. **length()**: Returns the size of the file in bytes.
5. **renameTo()**: Renames a file or directory.
6. **isDirectory()**: Checks if the file is a directory.
7. **isFile()**: Checks if the file is a regular file.
8. **canRead()**: Checks if the file is readable.
9. **canWrite()**: Checks if the file is writable.
10. **list()**: Lists the names of files in a directory.

Example:

```
import java.io.File;

public class FileMethodsExample {
    public static void main(String[] args) {
        File file = new File("testfile.txt");

        if (file.exists()) {
            System.out.println("File exists: " + file.getName());
            System.out.println("File size: " + file.length() + " bytes");
            System.out.println("Can read: " + file.canRead());
            System.out.println("Can write: " + file.canWrite());
        } else {
            System.out.println("File does not exist.");
        }
    }
}
```

---

6. Question: What is the role of exception handling in file operations? Explain with an example how `try-catch` blocks are used for file handling.

Answer:
Exception handling plays a crucial role in file operations because file I/O operations are prone to errors due to reasons such as file not being found, insufficient permissions, or I/O interruptions. Java provides a robust exception handling mechanism using `try-catch` blocks to handle such exceptions gracefully.

When performing file operations, we wrap the code in a `try` block and catch specific exceptions such as `FileNotFoundException`, `IOException`, or `AccessDeniedException`. This ensures that any errors encountered during file reading or writing are caught, and the program doesn't crash unexpectedly.

Example:

```
import java.io.FileReader;
import java.io.IOException;

public class ExceptionHandlingExample {
```

```
    public static void main(String[] args) {
        try {
            FileReader fr = new FileReader("nonexistent.txt");
        } catch (IOException e) {
            System.out.println("An error occurred: " + e.getMessage());
            e.printStackTrace();
        }
    }
}
```

In this example:

- The program tries to open a file (nonexistent.txt) that does not exist.
- An IOException is caught, and a message is displayed without crashing the program.

---

7. Question: Explain the difference between FileInputStream and FileReader in Java.

Answer:
Both FileInputStream and FileReader are used for reading files in Java, but they differ in the type of data they handle:

1. **FileInputStream**:
   - It is used to read **binary data** from a file.
   - It reads the file byte by byte and can be used for reading any type of file (text files, image files, audio files, etc.).
   - Suitable for non-text files.
2. **FileReader**:
   - It is used to read **character data** from a file.
   - It reads the file character by character, making it suitable for reading text files.
   - It automatically handles the encoding and decoding of text (e.g., UTF-8, ASCII).

Example of FileInputStream:

```
import java.io.FileInputStream;
import java.io.IOException;

public class FileInputStreamExample {
    public static void main(String[] args) {
        try {
            FileInputStream fis = new FileInputStream("image.jpg");
            int byteData;
            while ((byteData = fis.read()) != -1) {
                System.out.print((char) byteData);
            }
            fis.close();
        } catch (IOException e) {
            System.out.println("Error reading binary file");
```

```
            }
        }
    }
```

8. Question: How do you list the contents of a directory in Java? Provide an example.

Answer:
In Java, to list the contents of a directory, we use the `list()` method of the `File` class. This method returns an array of filenames (as strings) of the files and directories in the specified directory.

Example:

```java
import java.io.File;

public class ListDirectoryContents {
    public static void main(String[] args) {
        File directory = new File(".");

        if (directory.exists() && directory.isDirectory()) {
            String[] files = directory.list();
            for (String file : files) {
                System.out.println(file);
            }
        } else {
            System.out.println("Directory not found or is not a directory.");
        }
    }
}
```

This code lists all the files and subdirectories in the current directory.

9. Question: What is the role of `RandomAccessFile` in Java file handling? How does it differ from other file I/O classes?

Answer:
`RandomAccessFile` is a special class in Java that allows for **random access** to files. Unlike other file I/O classes, which only allow sequential reading or writing, `RandomAccessFile` allows reading or writing at any position in the file.

Key Features:

- **Seek operations**: You can move the file pointer to any position using the `seek()` method, enabling random access to data.
- **File manipulation**: You can read and write data at any point in the file.

- **Read and write modes**: `RandomAccessFile` can be opened in "read" or "read-write" mode.

Example:

```java
import java.io.RandomAccessFile;
import java.io.IOException;

public class RandomAccessFileExample {
    public static void main(String[] args) {
        try {
            RandomAccessFile file = new RandomAccessFile("data.txt", "rw");

            // Writing to file
            file.writeUTF("Hello, world!");

            // Moving to the start of the file
            file.seek(0);
            System.out.println(file.readUTF());

            file.close();
        } catch (IOException e) {
            System.out.println("An error occurred.");
        }
    }
}
```

`RandomAccessFile` is useful for applications such as database systems where accessing specific records in a file is required.

---

10. Question: What is the difference between `FileWriter` and `BufferedWriter` in Java? When should one use BufferedWriter over FileWriter?

Answer:
Both `FileWriter` and `BufferedWriter` are used to write text to files, but they serve slightly different purposes.

1. **FileWriter**:
   - `FileWriter` writes characters directly to the file.
   - It does not provide any buffering. Every write operation results in a direct write to the disk, which may lead to inefficiencies when writing large amounts of data.
2. **BufferedWriter**:
   - `BufferedWriter` provides buffering to the data being written.
   - It improves performance by writing data to a memory buffer before actually writing it to the file. This reduces the number of disk access operations.

When to use BufferedWriter:

- When you are writing large amounts of text to a file.
- When you want to reduce the overhead of frequent disk access.

Example of Using BufferedWriter:

```java
import java.io.FileWriter;
import java.io.BufferedWriter;
import java.io.IOException;

public class BufferedWriterExample {
    public static void main(String[] args) {
        try {
            FileWriter fileWriter = new FileWriter("output.txt");
            BufferedWriter bufferedWriter = new BufferedWriter(fileWriter);

            bufferedWriter.write("This is a large text written
efficiently.");
            bufferedWriter.close();
        } catch (IOException e) {
            System.out.println("An error occurred.");
        }
    }
}
```

In this example, `BufferedWriter` improves writing performance when handling larger files.